MASTERS AT WORK

BECOMING A NEUROSURGEON

BECOMING A VETERINARIAN

BECOMING A VENTURE CAPITALIST

BECOMING A HAIRSTYLIST

BECOMING A REAL ESTATE AGENT

BECOMING A MARINE BIOLOGIST

BECOMING AN ETHICAL HACKER

BECOMING A LIFE COACH

MASTERS AT WORK

BECOMING
A BAKER

GLYNNIS MACNICOL

SIMON & SCHUSTER

New York   London   Toronto   Sydney   New Delhi

Simon & Schuster
1230 Avenue of the Americas
New York, NY 10020

First Simon & Schuster hardcover edition September 2019

SIMON & SCHUSTER and colophon are registered trademarks
of Simon & Schuster, Inc.

For information about special discounts for bulk purchases, please contact
Simon & Schuster Special Sales at 1-866-506-1949 or
business@simonandschuster.com.

The Simon & Schuster Speakers Bureau can bring authors to your live event.
For more information or to book an event contact the
Simon & Schuster Speakers Bureau at 1-866-248-3049 or visit
our website at www.simonspeakers.com.

Manufactured in the United States of America

1   3   5   7   9   10   8   6   4   2

Library of Congress Cataloging-in-Publication Data is available.

ISBN 978-1-9821-2027-6
ISBN 978-1-9821-2028-3 (ebook)

FOR THE *M*'s, OF COURSE

CONTENTS

1. Ladybird   1

2. The History of Baking   17

3. A Day of Baking   31

4. The Brooklyn Blackout   45

5. Becoming a Baker   55

6. A.D. *SATC*   77

7. I Don't Smell Anything   91

8. The Future of Baking   113

   Appendix   127

BECOMING
A BAKER

———

1

LADYBIRD

It's 1:00 p.m. on a Tuesday in February in Park Slope, Brooklyn. A bitter wind barrels down the nearly empty sidewalks of Eighth Avenue. This is the quiet hour. Lunchtime is over and the schools won't let out for another two hours, spilling students onto the sidewalks and into the local diners and coffee shops. Weather forecasters are predicting a winter storm for tomorrow, and there's the slightly ominous feeling in the air of a city preparing to batten down.

Park Slope has a reputation for many things, but tops among them is that it is a neighborhood for families. If New York City is essentially a cluster of small towns—each with its own history, customs, and rules; grouped together in a tiny space; and connected by subway lines instead of highways—Park Slope has long been the place couples with small children leave the city for when they don't actually want to leave the city. These days, real estate prices are such that relocations like this are largely limited to millionaires, but the neighborhood still manages to maintain a seventies, *Sesame Street* vibe despite the influx of money. This is the epicenter of Brooklyn's brownstone-lined streets, the heart of New York's liberal leanings. Mayor Bill de Blasio has called it home for decades, and still makes the trip all the way from Gracie Mansion on the Upper East Side to exercise at the local YMCA every day. Senator Chuck Schumer's downstate residence is in one of the handful of prewar apartment buildings that line Prospect Park a few blocks away. Park Slope's legendary food co-op—founded in the early seventies by residents who wanted access to good food—is one of the oldest and largest in the nation; it's also notorious for strict membership rules that have generated near-mythical stories around the city over the years.

Eighth Avenue runs between bustling Seventh Avenue, the neighborhood's main street, and Prospect Park West, which borders the west side of the park. Prospect Park is Brooklyn's version of Central Park, minus the tourists and the fences needed to prevent them from ruining the grass. In the summer, the park is the borough's enormous bustling backyard, hosting barbecues, drum circles, picnics, and concerts. Right now, it's mostly empty save for a few resolute joggers and cyclists taking advantage of its emptier hours. If the forecasted storm brings actual snow tomorrow, then the Long Meadow will become host to a serious sledding scene, but for now everything remains gray and cold.

Eighth Avenue is almost entirely residential. From where it begins off Grand Army Plaza to where it ends a mile and a half south at the Prospect Expressway before continuing to and merging with Fort Hamilton Parkway, it's a long series of brownstone stoops and apartment entries, interspersed with a few churches and synagogues from one end to the other, save for a pocket of blink-and-you-might-miss small stores between Eleventh and Twelfth Streets that somehow slipped through the zoning laws. This pocket of stores is so easily missed, in fact, that when one gets off the F or G train exit at the corner of Ninth Street and Eighth Avenue and begins walking south, there is almost always a moment of panic just past the corner of Tenth Street: *Is it still there? Does it look closed? Has it packed up and disappeared like so many other beloved New York businesses?* But then you cross Eleventh Street and you sigh from relief. *It's* still there. Along with the small spa, taco place, and pizza bar on the far

Ladybird Bakery

corner. There right in the middle, the narrow blue awning now visible, thank goodness, is Ladybird Bakery.

Ladybird is tiny. Small even by New York standards, it has a quaint mom-and-pop appearance that so many new businesses try to capture, except here it's underdone in a way that reinforces its authenticity. The patina has been earned, not created. A simple sky-blue awning hangs over the door, displaying the name LADYBIRD in contained letters that are barely readable a block away (hence the repeated panic that comes with every visit). On either end of the awning are the bakery's address and phone number. The phone number hints to its longstanding presence in the neighborhood; a throwback to when people *called* to place their order, rather than doing it online. The windows are rimmed with paintings of wildflowers. On either side of the door are plain wooden benches that invite loitering; despite its small footprint, customers are invited to take up as much space as they can.

Once inside, the narrow room is dominated by a large glass display case that is brimming with baked goods. Like suddenly stepping into a bright light, it can take a few minutes to make sense of everything that is being offered. To the left are all the tarts and pies, on the right are all the cakes—each shelf devoted to a different size and flavor. On top of the counter are plates of cookies, muffins, and, if you get there early enough, scones. The floor behind the counter is elevated, so the servers can better see the customers, but even with their added height, the servers still have to peer at customers through the tall plates of baked goods piled on the counter. Opposite the counter are a handful of tables pushed against the windows, enough to sit two to three people each. In the morning, these tables are filled with young schoolchildren and their parents; around 3:00 p.m., they are crowded with high school students stopping by for a snack.

Once your eye adjusts to the bonanza of baked goods—the cakes with different icings and colorful decorations are especially dazzling—it slowly becomes apparent that there are few actual signs marking what's what. There are no price tags at all. *You must ask.* It's at this stage of the purchasing process that it becomes especially easy to spot the regular from the newbie. Those who point with assurance when called upon—*the six-inch Blackout, please*—and those who pause, frown, and then begin a series of familiar questions: *What's in that cake? How much does the small one cost? How many inches is the big one? Can I have it personalized?* Ladybird is a place that requires conversation.

THE DESIRE TO CONNECT is perhaps the thing that defines a baker more than anything else. Baking is about enjoyment, whether it be in celebration or simply end-of-day comfort. More precisely, baking is about *other* people's enjoyment. Chefs can happily make a meal for one, but no one bakes for themselves. Is there another profession so devoted to bringing happiness to other people's lives? It's difficult to imagine a simpler, more direct way to bring some goodness into the world on a daily basis.

At the moment, Ladybird is empty except for Mary Louise Clemens, Ladybird's owner, who has just arrived and is sitting at the corner table scrolling through her phone. Clemens opened Ladybird (then called Two Little Red Hens), in this space twenty-five years ago, and has been its sole owner for the last thirteen. Running a small, brick-and-mortar business anywhere in the country could reasonably be considered an act of insanity in the digital age, but to do so in New York for more than a quarter century *successfully* is a combination of heroic and miraculous. And yet, perhaps there's no better measure of how well Clemens's bakery is run than the fact she's able to show up at 1:00 p.m. and immediately launch into a topic that has nothing to do with baked goods at all. She's currently obsessed with another feel-good activity: the Westminster Kennel Club Dog Show.

Clemens is a cheerful woman in her mid-fifties, with a round youthful face, bobbed brown hair, and glasses. If you pay very close attention when she speaks, you can hear traces of a Southern accent when she pronounces certain words. She's wearing a vest over her button-down shirt and jeans; if it wasn't the middle of winter in Brooklyn, you might well assume her hobby is gardening, not attending dog shows. A snow advisory has just officially been issued for New York

City beginning at 5:00 a.m. tomorrow, but Clemens, who is scrolling through her phone, looking for pictures from last year's event, will not be deterred. Pier 94, where the show is being held, is on the westernmost side of the city, part of a neighborhood that for decades housed working docks but not much else and is subsequently a no-man's-land of public transportation with the nearest subway four avenues away. Last year, Clemens was sporting an injured foot and slogged the whole way in an orthopedic boot. "It was worth it," she says. But she's already decided not to walk in tomorrow's snow. This year she'll take the train into Manhattan and then a taxi the remaining blocks to Pier 94.

She returns to her dog pictures to point out one of last year's contestants in the boxer category. "It's just so crazy. This poor guy, I mean he had just a normal little coat, but all these other ones are decked out and look like Elvis," she says, and I can catch her faint accent when she says the musician's name. She scrolls again. "And this is my dog watching the dog show that night. She loves to watch TV."

IF YOU WERE ABLE to follow Clemens's Southern accent back to its origin, it would lead you to San Angelo, Texas, a small city ninety minutes south of Abilene, where she was born and raised. No one who knew her then would be surprised at what she was doing now. "I started baking when I was a child because I didn't want to do yard work in Texas," says Clemens. "My friends would come over and I would pretend I had a bakery. I started off using Bisquick and different things like that. My parents would wake up and I'd have the whole table filled with stuff. It was crazy."

At twelve, she took her first cake-decorating class at the local college, learning the basics like flowers and seashells. She was so young, her mother had to enroll with her. By age fifteen, she knew that baking was her calling. "I could have stayed up all night doing other things, I suppose, though this was the seventies in mid-Texas so you didn't really have other things. You didn't have TV, or TV was not like it is now, so that's what we did."

At nineteen, she enrolled in San Angelo State to study management and emerged with an associate's degree. Following that, she enrolled in the Culinary Institute of America. The Culinary Institute, "the other CIA" as many of its students jokingly refer to it, opened in 1946 as the New Haven Restaurant Institute and was designed to train returning veterans in the culinary arts. In his memoir *Kitchen*

Confidential, Anthony Bourdain devotes an entire chapter to his time there in the mid-seventies, crediting it, in a round-about way, as the thing that readied in him for the cooking world. A sort of military basic training, but for cooking.

Like many of its graduates in those days, when Clemens left she immediately landed a job, through CIA connections, at a hotel in California. The hotel was on the edge of Monterey Bay, and Clemens was hired onto the small pastry team. Hotel desserts are plated affairs. "It's a different kind of dessert than what you'd do for a bakery, unless it's for a buffet," notes Clemens. "You rarely make an entire cake." But she loved it. "It was a gorgeous hotel. I would do the plated desserts, or desserts for a buffet, and things like that. So, I worked there for a couple of years and then I moved to another hotel in another part of California."

Though she didn't see herself working in a hotel for the long-term, she's quick to credit her time there for helping her develop strengths she still relies on today. First and foremost, time management. "I learned how to set up a buffet, how to put out two hundred desserts on a strict time-table. You know, in an hour or ten minutes if you have to get it plated up. It teaches you that kind of skill, how to be fast and organize your time, and just make things happen."

It also taught her the skill of presentation, which was helpful when Ladybird got into wholesale and was doing large events for clients like the Brooklyn Botanic Garden. "I needed dessert for five hundred people and I knew I had the skills to do that kind of volume."

After these initial years on the hotel circuit, Clemens transitioned to a small bakery in the area that was even smaller than Ladybird. It was here she learned how to decorate specialty cakes. "At the CIA we learned to decorate but it wasn't the same." She was still in her twenties at this point, benefitting enormously from the people she was working with. So what could compel a Texan, whose professional life had thus far happily existed in the beautiful surroundings of Monterey Bay, California, to relocate to eighties New York City, a place then overwhelmed with crime and battling a crack epidemic?

Two words: cheap rent.

BY THE TIME SHE moved to the city, Clemens had married a New Yorker and her husband had a rent-controlled apartment on the Upper West Side. Even in the eighties rent-controlled apartments were not easy to come by; when they separated not long after, Clemens managed to keep the apartment, which made all the difference in her ability to live in New York and pursue baking on her own terms. "I was paying five hundred dollars a month rent for a one-bedroom on the Upper West Side. That's how I was able to survive," she says bluntly.

It was during this period of adjustment that Clemens started her own business with friend Christina Winkler. "She was a little bit older and had kids. I was young, soon to be single, and no kids. She kept on talking about doing something and I was like, 'Well, let's do it.'" In the beginning, that "something" was simply selling their wares out of the back of Clemens's van. They would bake for hours in either Clemens's apartment or Winkler's mother's kitchen on the Upper East Side, then drive the goods down to the St. Mark's farmers market in the East Village.

In the beginning, it was tough going. Clemens, like previous generations of New York newcomers trying to make it in the city, lived on baked potatoes, sometimes with cheese and pesto if she had the leftover money to buy the additional ingredients. She and Winkler added another farmers market to their rounds and did all their baking themselves. They named their business Two Little Red Hens. "We wanted 'The Little Red Hen,'" says Clemens, "but that was taken, actually, I think by an Italian place or a pizza place or a chicken place. I'm not even sure. It was taken so we couldn't do it, so another friend said, 'There's two of you so just go with two,' and so we did that."

After a year they moved their baking to a shared kitchen owned by a woman for whom Clemens had worked briefly when she first came to New York. This was the early nineties; *Frasier* had just premiered on prime time, introducing the world to the idea that drinking coffee with long fancy names was a sophisticated pastime. Coffee bars were beginning to open up around the city, and Clemens and Winkler began supplying pastries to one on the Upper East Side. "It was opened by a girl who was from Seattle and she had some family money backing. That was our first wholesale account."

Not long after, in 1994, they decided it was time to take the plunge and open their own doors. They began searching for a location that might work. Location mattered less, remembers Clemens, than simply fulfilling the need to have their own space. "Brooklyn or Manhattan, we didn't care." Baker friends gave her a list of bakeries to visit, including a spot way down on Eighth Avenue in Brooklyn. At the time it housed a bakery called Faith's, owned by a woman of the same name. In 1994, *The New York Times* called it a "gem of a shop" and as far back as 1988 the paper was championing its "excellent sweet potato, pecan, and cranberry lattice pies."

It was somewhat out of the way, but Clemens and Winkler went and looked anyway. They took it immediately, which as any person who has hunted for property in New York will tell you is the only way to get anything.

"We walked in, looked around, and that was it," recalls Clemens. "It was very lucky, because the owners were going to close, but we came in at the last minute and got it." Clemens borrowed $30,000 from her mother to cover her half of the start-up costs (over the next few years she repaid it entirely, plus 7.5 percent interest). But even with the loan, it was still a hard time. "I mean, I had nothing. I was newly divorced and single. I only paid five hundred dollars in rent but I scraped [by]. It was very, very hard for me."

Like so much in the city, the neighborhood they settled in has changed drastically over the years; the space they landed between Eleventh and Twelfth Streets was then considered the outskirts of Park Slope. While these days it's prime Park Slope territory, two decades ago it was still considered somewhat of a risk, business-wise. "Twelfth Street was the dividing line when we first came," says Clemens. "The Realtors would come by and point to 'the little bakery' as a selling point."

Happily, the pair didn't have to start from scratch. Included in the sale from Faith's was much of the machinery, along with a series of her recipes—including one for the Brooklyn Blackout. The new owners immediately scrapped it. Faith had other things that were very good, but her recipe for the Brooklyn Blackout "was not one of them," Clemens recalls. It would be years before the Blackout reappeared on Eighth Avenue. Instead, for a long time Two Little Red Hens stuck to the breakfast items it'd sold at the farmers market: scones, cupcakes, and muffins.

"The first couple of years we were here we didn't sell any decorated cakes at all; there wasn't really the market for that yet," Clemens explains. This would change in the next few years, largely due to one very famous cupcake.

2

THE HISTORY OF BAKING

For most of history, the role of a baker needed no explanation. It's an occupation—or perhaps, more accurately, a vocation—so established, and so relatively unchanging, that it makes appearances in both the Bible, as well as centuries-old children's rhymes (butchers we still have; candlestick makers, not so much). Fast-forward to the present day and baking also features prominently in twenty-first-century reality shows. It's hard to think of another profession (one that's legal, anyway) that can claim such a constant, largely unchanging presence in our shared history. Let's define it anyway: Baking, simply put, means using dry heat to cook food.

You'd need a book the length of an encyclopedia to properly detail the entire history of baking around the world; each culture has its own traditions, local ingredients, and environments that determine how and what gets made. (As anyone who has tried to bake a cake on a humid day with no AC, or say, at a mountain cabin can tell you, environment is a key element of baking.) Here, instead, is a brief look at some major developments that have led up to where we are today.

In the beginning baked food primarily meant bread, which humans have been making for thousands of years. The world's oldest oven, discovered in what is now Croatia, dates to 6500 BCE, though archaeologists have also found evidence of baking among the earliest evidence of human activity. For early civilizations, "baking" largely comprised mashed grains compacted with water and cooked over a fire. Over time, sweeteners such as honey and maple syrup were added, and ingredients branched out to include more than basic grains. Unleavened bread, bread that is prepared without a raising agent, was and remains a staple in many cultures. It factors heavily into Passover as matzo, for instance; the Christian Eucharist is an unleavened wafer. Warmer countries have the tortilla and roti is common in South Asia.

The Egyptians are widely considered to have discovered yeast—likely as a leftover from making beer—and were in-

White Sourdough from Sea Wolf Bakery

spired to add it to bread. This was the first rising agent. Fermented grain was also used as a leavener, which is what creates the distinctly tangy taste of sourdough bread. "For hundreds of years, yeast is primarily how things were leavened. And sourdough as well: the starters, the naturally created, fermented grain that makes sourdough," says cake historian Jessica Reed, author of the book *The Baker's Appendix.*

The Greeks introduced closed ovens, and by the time the Roman Empire rolled in, being a baker, or pastry chef—Romans, who gave a new meaning to the term gluttony, liked their sweets—was an actual job.

"You start seeing a major transition around the Middle Ages," says Reed. As more spices and sugars from China, India, and Africa began to make their way along trade routes and into Europe, "an expanded repertoire develops." It was also during this time that people began using eggs as a leavener, though as Reed notes, more eggs were needed in those days because they were much smaller compared to modern ones. "Think twenty eggs whipped for an hour to make a leavener, as opposed to the ten that would be needed today." Additionally, baking began to move from primarily bread to more biscuit products, and sweet things closer to what we think of as cakes were slowly introduced. Custards were popular, often sweetened with honey and wine. Ginger and pine nuts were popular ingredients.

IT WASN'T UNTIL THE late eighteenth century, however, that baking underwent significant changes, and those were "stratospheric," says Reed. "The inventions and developments during this time led to the ability to make baked goods, particularly cakes, as we do today." In 1775, the French Academy of Sciences held a competition, offering a prize to the person who could figure how to produce soda ash, also known as sodium carbonate, from salt. French chemist Nicolas Leblanc took on the challenge, and by 1791 had successfully figured out a two-step process to do so. After his discovery, sodium bicarbonate, commonly known as baking soda, was created and quickly became the first popular transitive leavener. In 1843, a British chemist named Alfred Bird, intent on finding an alternate leavening agent for his wife who was allergic to yeast, invented the first iteration of what would come to be known as baking powder by combining baking soda with cream of tartar (a residue left over after winemaking . . . baking owes a long debt of gratitude to alcohol by-products). For Americans, however, cream of tartar was an expensive item that needed to be shipped overseas from Europe, which kept it out of the hands of poorer bakers. Hoping to discover a different, less expensive way to create the same product, Harvard professor Eben Horsford reformulated baking powder by boiling down beef and mutton bones to extract monocalcium phosphate. He then combined the compound with baking soda to create an alternate version of baking powder. In 1856 he patented this formula, and began making it available in stores. Not long after, he simplified things by adding cornstarch, and modern baking powder was invented.

It's difficult to overstate the impact of this discovery on the lives of bakers—entire books have been devoted to the "Baking Powder Wars." This is especially true for women, who were the primary bakers for their households. Women were often judged on their ability to bake bread, their worth tied to its outcome. Prior to the invention of baking powder, baking was something that was generally done once a week because of the amount of preparation required to make the outcome successful: the fire had to be heated to a specific temperature and kept stable for long periods of time, yeast was unreliable, and the dough had to be left out to rise. Villagers might use a communal oven, making the dough at home and then taking it into town to bake there. The arrival of baking powder fundamentally changed this lengthy ritual, and domination for the market became fierce. By 1896, Americans were consuming almost 120 pounds of baking powder annually. The ingredient also shifted baked goods, particularly those that were sweeter, from being something wealthier people, who had access to both expensive sugar and means to employ labor, enjoyed to something increasingly accessible to the lower classes. Now, instead of the heavy, biscuity baked goods that had been so common, cakes became lighter and airier, more closely resembling what we now think of as cakes and cookies.

In addition to the advent of baking powder came a number of other equally influential creations. In the late eighteenth century the iron oven, fired by coal or wood, was invented, moving baking away from the traditional hearth and allowing for more control over temperature and distribution of heat. Also in the eighteenth and nineteenth centuries, developments were made in refrigeration, which allowed bakers to store ingredients; they no longer had to worry about milk souring, for instance, or constant access to fresh eggs (fun fact: eggs used to be a "seasonal crop" since hens often stopped laying in the winter). This also had a significant effect on commercial bakers, who were becoming increasingly popular as women began moving away from the home and into the workplace following the Industrial Revolution.

The next "burst of change," as Reed calls it, happened with the invention of universal measurements in the late nineteenth century. Recipes had existed as far back as the sixteenth century, but they were mostly devoid of measurements or instructions. Instead, instructions were passed down from mother to daughter over many generations and were comprised of a list of ingredients: twelve eggs, a handful of sugar, etc., but nothing else (ironically, these are now just the sorts of instructions employed on reality baking shows). "Girls stood and watched," says Reed. "They had to; you were the daughter and that's what daughters did. They didn't go to school; they stayed home and they cleaned and they cooked with their mother." This changed with the arrival of a woman named Fannie Farmer.

Born in 1857 to an upper-class family in Boston, Massachusetts, Farmer's education was thwarted by a stroke she suffered at the age of sixteen. During the years she was convalescing at her parents' home she taught herself to cook. By the age of thirty she had recovered her ability to walk again and enrolled at the Boston Cooking School. Her time there coincided with the heyday of the domestic science movement, which introduced "home economics" as a field of study for women and included courses on nutrition, diet, and health standards in cooking. Farmer relished her time at the school and took a position as principal of the school after graduating. In 1896, she published *The Boston Cooking-School Cook Book*, which introduced standardized measurements—the teaspoon, the cup—and recipe writing that are still in use today. The book was a runaway success and, much to the surprise of its publisher Little, Brown and Company, which had authorized an initial printing of only three thousand copies, remains in print today.

This opened baking up to anyone who could access a recipe, notes Reed. "You didn't have to learn it from your mother. That was the forefront of home economics and training women . . . in the art of home care. And not just as servants, but as the wife, the mother, the person that lived in the house."

On the heels of Farmer, came the KitchenAid stand mixer. As the digital age increasingly encroaches on our everyday life, we love to fetishize the homemade and the artisanal, however, up until the early twentieth century, baking, washing, and cleaning were all labor-intensive, full-day events. It's not hard to imagine how welcome, desperate even, women would be for a reprieve and how significantly their quality of life might be changed by the introduction of something as simple as a machine that could *do* the mixing and kneading for you. This is what a man by the name of Herbert Johnson had in mind when he created the H mixer. Produced by the Hobart Corporation, the H mixer was initially invented for industrial use and was installed on a number of American battleships during World War I. In 1918 it was developed for home use and the KitchenAid home model was introduced. (We have the Great War to thank for a number of modern "conveniences:" the disposable razor was developed for soldiers in the field, and when the war ended the surplus was introduced to the public.) In the beginning, stores had to be convinced to carry the H mixer—the early version was both heavy (weighing in at sixty-five pounds) and expensive ($189, the equivalent of $2800 today). Hobart's solution to this challenge was to enlist all-women sales teams to go door-to-door selling the mixers. A decade later, a smaller, lighter version, the G model, was introduced and was an immediate hit, owing in part to increased access to electricity in American homes. This shrinking and lightening continued to be the trend for the next ten years as the K model, though production was halted entirely during World War II.

The arrival of the mixer overlaps with what Reed calls an interesting time in baking, particularly with cakes. "After these huge changes in the nineteenth and the early twentieth century, not much has changed when it comes to cake. Textures have shifted a bit because of the KitchenAid mixer; you can get an airier cake than you could back then because you're not doing everything by hand. But again, as it was with the first thousand, five hundred years, you have these bursts of change and then you have a long period of kind of just rolling with it how it is."

At this point, cakes start to become more about the decorating and less about the contents, though there was some precedent for this at least; the cakes on Queen Victoria's royal tables, particularly the "showstoppers" as they are known, were created to be regarded rather than consumed. Even so, they were perhaps better described as "sugar sculptures," says Reed; the actual cakes that were eaten were much smaller and were "heavy with booze and heavy with sugar," which both act as preservatives. But these too were made to last. Think here of the famous British pound cakes that in addition to being baked with heavy amounts of sugar and alcohol are then wrapped in a liquor-soaked cheesecloth to boot. Afterward, they'd be put in a tin where they might last for a couple of months, if not longer.

The mid-twentieth century's new push toward decorating, however, was less boozy and more edible. In the fifties and sixties, as women were being pushed back into the home after the war, advertising leaned heavily on the "perfect homemaker" as a selling point, pressuring real women to achieve a similar standard. Baking-powder companies, chocolate companies, and cocoa companies began creating pamphlets that would allow customers to purchase the actual cakes cheaply at the grocery store. Additionally, these pamphlets also included recipes for how to use their other products in order to decorate the cakes at home. Says Reed, "You begin seeing women at home baking birthday cakes for their kids, and it starts becoming this cultural thing of a good mother, a good wife, knows how to bake a cake. You also start seeing women doing more of the decorating of cakes, making cakes shaped like a lamb or something for a birthday."

It was into this world that Julia Child and her television show arrived, bringing baking and cooking into the home in an entirely new, and far more personal way. Before branching into television, Child, of course, had coauthored the legendary two-volume *Mastering the Art of French Cooking*, which introduced French cuisine and cooking techniques to the American household. Two years later, Child debuted *The French Chef*, which she created and starred in. It was one of the first cooking shows on American television, and quickly reached iconic status, in part because of Child's delivery—her voice was particularly notable—and in part because it was filmed live and subsequently aired unedited (she became equally beloved and notorious for her gaffes). One might argue in addition to being the first mainstream cooking show it was also America's first reality TV show. In her determination to make cooking, baking, and the more difficult art of making pastries accessible to the everyday chef, Child also demonstrated that cooking could be just as compelling as any other form of entertainment. Neither she nor anyone else could have imagined how popular her show would be from this simple revelation. Or that within a few decades there would be entire networks devoted to culinary shows, and various cooking and baking competitions.

3

A DAY OF BAKING

Roman arrives each day at Ladybird at 3:00 a.m. He travels here from his home in Ditmas Park—a neighborhood approximately three miles south, just across Prospect Park—where he has lived since arriving in the city thirty years ago as a teenager. In any other place this would be considered an ideal commute, particularly with the lack of traffic at such an early hour, but because the designers of the New York City subway system did not envision that a century later the city's inhabitants would take the train anywhere but to Manhattan and back, Roman's simple trip is nearly an hour in each direction and involves two subway lines.

The first thing Roman does when he gets to the bakery is to immediately check the board hanging inside the kitchen for tickets detailing special orders: wedding cakes, birthday cakes, special occasion cakes of varying sizes and flavors.

These will be incorporated into his already packed schedule: in addition to making sure the case out front is stocked, there are also orders to be filled for Union Market, a local grocery store that has three locations in Brooklyn and sells Ladybird's cakes and cupcakes, as well as a bagel store on Seventh Avenue, which sells scones and muffins.

There are almost always special orders. Ladybird's website has a page detailing all the cake options available to customers—and it's extensive. There are ten cakes to choose from, twenty-two fillings, and seventeen frostings. The page includes a note that the bakery needs forty-eight to seventy-two hours' notice for orders (and suggests that one full week is ideal for tiered cakes). There is no online order form. Orders at Ladybird are accepted only over the phone and are handwritten by one of the (invariably) young people working behind the counter. The online custom-cake menu is, to some degree, merely just a detailed nod to our digitized way of life, as well as a stab at keeping questions about cake, filling, and frosting combinations to a minimum (though Vicky, who will work the counter later that morning, tells me it often just leads to additional questions and strange cake-flavor fusions). This lack of internet savvy is perhaps Ladybird's own best advertisement for itself; its roots run so deep in the real-life community that establishing an online presence was an afterthought; something a college student who works summers behind the counter might have offered to do, but was never actually necessary. People *want* to come here in person.

AFTER CHECKING THE TICKETS, Roman moves on to the mixing. The tasks in the kitchen have all been separated among the employees; Roman is in charge of batters, and he has the day's requirements listed in shorthand on a clipboard on the table next to his workstation. Dark Chocolate is at the top, underlined. Below it are numbers corresponding to the width of the cakes he needs: one twelve-inch, one fourteen-inch, etc. Below that is the same again for Yellow cake. Below that is another list: Red Velvet, Dark Chocolate, Carrot. The page appears strikingly blank considering the baking output, and Roman is currently the only person here prepping for the day. I ask him if he has all the recipes memorized. He shrugs and gives me a self-deprecating smile: "Some of them."

Roman has a patient, sweet nature and a face to match, both of which belie his forty-five years. When he was fourteen, he moved to New York City from Mexico with his father and has worked in the bakery ever since. Or, to be more accurate, in a bakery at this location. Roman started at Faith's, the bakery that Clemens and Winkler purchased, as a dishwasher, opting out of attending school to work because he needed to pay rent. After the first few years, Faith began teaching him the basics of baking, starting with cookies and muffins. For the next five to seven years—"It begins to blur together," he says with a rueful grin—he worked as both a dishwasher and baker: "Nobody wanted to do dishes, so I did both." After Faith sold the bakery, he stayed on the staff and moved to baking full-time. For a long time he used to do everything, but as the bakery became busier the duties were eventually split up.

While we talk, he begins cracking eggs over a bowl and separating the whites from the yolks with his hands. The whites remain in the bowl to be whipped while the yolks get tossed into a large Tupperware container that will go in the fridge for later use. Behind us, Yellow cakes of various sizes are baking in three different tiered ovens. When the timer dings, Roman opens the oven doors and rotates the cakes. He tells me he normally makes thirty cakes at a time (Ladybird sells "a few hundred" cakes each week, according to Clemens). As I watch him go back to cracking eggs, I ask him how many eggs he goes through in a day. Each day is different, he says, but a hundred eggs are needed for each batch of cake batter, and he makes four batches every three days. This means Ladybird uses nearly a thousand eggs each week.

Ladybird has a small kitchen, maybe three hundred square feet. Along one wall are four ovens and a large fridge. On the back wall stands an army of mixers. Down the center are three aluminum-topped workstations, separated by shelves. In the near corner, a swinging door leads to the narrow back counter behind the cake display; opposite that, a staircase leads to the basement. The basement contains a walk-in fridge and freezer, storage space for all the boxes, a small rail for coats, and additional workspace for Edgar, the baker who is responsible for the fillings and the frostings. *Frosting*, not *icing*—no one ices things here; they frost.

The timer goes off again. Roman smoothly pulls out a tray of smaller, eight-inch cakes and slides it onto the trolley to cool. He moves around the confined space so seamlessly one wonders if he even needs to look where he's going. A big mixer in the back has been slowly churning while we've been talking. He turns it off, unhooks the large bowl from its base, and places it on top of what looks like a large rubber garbage can back at his workstation. When I move over slightly, I can see it's actually a container marked FLOUR. The sleeves of his flannel shirt are already rolled up, so there's no hesitation as he plunges his arm into the bowl all the way past his elbow, mixing the batter by hand over and over, throwing his entire body weight into it. It's nearly 7:30 a.m. Roman has been here for four and a half hours at this point, and I wonder how many times he's already done this arduous mixing today. What batch is he on? Judging by the cakes in the oven it's definitely not his first. He glances up at me as I watch him slowly mix his umpteenth batch of the morning and confirms what I've already noticed: "Nothing is mechanic here."

Even I, a person whose baking experience is limited to the Duncan Hines Devil's Food Cake Mix I make with my nephew, could have told you everything at Ladybird is "handmade." You can tell the difference when you eat it. It's the difference between a vintage clothing item and fast fashion off the rack. Between a massage and a painkiller. Perhaps we all possess some human, instinctive sense that "hands have been laid," but this is the first time I've really considered what the laying of those hands—and arms, elbows, back, and leg muscles; turned neck, knees, and grounded feet—costs the person who's doing the laying. This is hard work. This is construction. This is the definition of manual labor. The outcome of baking is prettier than masonry, and associated with a certain kind of decadence, but the process involves no less sweat or endurance than constructing a building out of brick and mortar. The more mechanized our culture gets, the more we fetishize the "natural." It takes about five minutes of watching Roman mix "by hand" to think how much more appealing the mechanic might be.

The intimacy of this labor really comes into focus when you consider just how much business Ladybird does instore; during the week, the bakery opens at 7:00 a.m. and five minutes later there is already a line at the counter comprising mostly parents walking their children to school.

At 8:30 a.m., Pedro arrives. Pedro is a heavyset man, with a serious face that frequently erupts into a big grin. Like Roman, he's been working here a long time—almost thirty years. In fact, all of Ladybird's bakers have been here for more than a decade if not longer. Once he puts down his coffee and a scone from the case in the café, he flips on a small mixer full of plain buttercream that's been chilling overnight in the fridge. He does this automatically, the way most people walk into a dark room and turn on the light. The motion of a mixer will bring the frosting up to room temperature without separating the ingredients, softening it enough for Pedro to spread on the cakes Roman has prepared. Pedro then puts a bowl of dark chocolate glaze over a pot on the stove to warm up. He is in charge of decorating and glazing, and his workstation is opposite Roman's.

It's busy out front. Peeking through the swinging door I spot two little girls sitting at one of the handful of small tables, backpacks on, licking the icing off their red velvet cupcakes, deeply unconcerned for the teachers who will be dealing with the aftermath of their inevitable sugar rush in an hour or so. Every ten minutes or so either Vicky or Shyran—the two women working the morning shift at the counter—come through the door with a small cake in hand, pop open the fridge behind Pedro's workstation, pull out one of the colored tubes of buttercream, and write something on the top of the cake. The four-inch cakes are too small for anything extensive, but can fit a heart or a letter. It's these tubes that Pedro now takes from the fridge and empties onto the counter, adding a scoop from the bowl of plain buttercream that has been mixing and spreading it expertly with a spatula until the color coheres. He pulls out a rectangular sheet of baking paper and quickly twists it up, matching the ends by instinct, twisting and folding until it becomes a tight tube. Then, with a graceful scoop of the spatula, the buttercream comes up off the table and is dropped into the tube. Pedro gives the bottom end of the tube a quick snip, and voilà: a fresh tube of buttercream for the day.

The table shows no evidence that, seconds before, it was covered in a thick layer of frosting. The speed and economy that has gone into creating a tube of buttercream that will decorate cakes for the rest of the day is impressive. The entire process took Pedro less than two minutes.

Pedro sees me gazing intently at his activity—it's difficult, after all, not to be aware of my presence in such a small space, which barely accommodates two grown men orchestrating the day's baked goods—and hands me a rectangular baking sheet to make my own tube. I struggle to line up the edges properly and keep the cylinder tight; this is harder than it looks. The results of my pastry tube, when I finally fold the last edge over and hand it back to Pedro, are haphazard at best. He glances at it, giving me a sympathetic smile. In the time it's taken me to come up with one shaky tube, he's replaced three more tubes and is in the process of replacing a fourth.

He's already emptied a tube of red buttercream onto the counter. Into this, he mixes a dollop of fresh white buttercream and adds a few drops of red dye, mixing it all up again and spreading it thin across the counter to make sure he has the right color consistency. Once it's mixed to his satisfaction, he scoops it all back up and drops it into my now mended paper tube.

GREGARIO, THE DISHWASHER, WHO at seven years has worked here the least amount of time, has now arrived and promptly dives into the mountain of mixing bowls that have piled up since the morning began.

On the opposite counter, Roman has pulled out a series of cupcake trays and filled them with oversize paper liners. He takes a large ice cream disher and begins filling the twelve compartments of each tray with batter he made this morning. Pedro maneuvers behind him to pull a tray of eight-inch unfrosted layer cakes from the fridge where they've been chilling overnight. He puts them down on his counter before returning to take the large bowl of dark chocolate off the pot where it's been heating on the stove.

The cakes he's about to glaze need to be cold, especially since the layers are separated with buttercream, which will melt if the temperature of the cakes is too warm. Pedro takes the bowl of glaze and pours it in a circular motion over each cake, letting the hot, dark chocolate drip down the sides. As I watch him, I remember the agonizing wait as a child between the cakes coming out of the oven and the moment when I could finally ice them. Once, my mother surrendered to my relentless pestering and let me ice the cake almost immediately after it came out of the oven. The result was big chunks of cake wrapped around balls of icing stuck to a knife. Delicious, yes, but obviously not servable.

It's nearly 9:00 a.m. In my regular life as a writer, much like anyone with a typical office job, I'd likely be sitting at my computer, responding to emails, scrolling through social media, and prepping for the day ahead, during which I may move to get lunch or refill my cup of coffee. The sum total of what I'd likely *make*, as in something that has a physical presence in the world, would already be in front of me in the form of coffee. Part of what is so satisfying about being in the bakery is watching things being physically created, step by step; from eggs being separated by hand and batter being mixed by arm to buttercream getting spread, dyed, and plopped into a hastily crafted paper tube. It sounds so incredibly basic. There is nothing mysterious about baking. Yet it is hard not to be struck by all ways that we are increasingly deprived of tangible, real-life craft, in a world that with each passing day exists more in "the cloud" than it does on the ground, while watching all these pieces come together knowing they will eventually result in something recognizable and beautiful (and, of course, delicious).

Roman slides the filled cupcake tins into the oven and brings over another crate of eggs. He stops to shade out the cakes on his list that he's already baked. I glance at the remaining items on his list, and see the word *chocolate* at the bottom. "Are you doing the Blackout now?" I ask, unable to keep the eagerness out of my voice. Roman shakes his head. More yellow batter. He must sense my disappointment. "You want to see Blackouts?" he asks. "Go downstairs and open the fridge on the left."

I follow his directions down the steep staircase; it's chillier down here, the cold February air hasn't been beaten back entirely by the heat from the ovens. I pass a workstation and open the walk-in fridge to the left. The first thing that hits me is the smell. A mixture of chocolate, sugar, and bread floats out to greet me. I recognize it immediately. It's a smell I associate with happiness. With significant holidays, important meals, and meaningful friendships. It smells like home, though not the home where I grew up—the home I made when I came to New York. It's the Brooklyn Blackout cake, and I am gazing upon rows and rows of them waiting to be frosted.

4

THE BROOKLYN BLACKOUT

In 2005, Nora Ephron wrote an essay for *The New York Times* titled "The Lost Strudel." It is an elegy for cabbage strudel, "which vanished from Manhattan in about 1982 and which I've been searching for these last twenty-three years," and a lament for a disappearing New York. She continues:

> This is New York, of course. The city throws curves. Rents go up. People get old, and their children no longer want to run the store. So you find yourself walking uptown looking for Mrs. Herbst's Hungarian bakery, which was there, has always been there, is a landmark for God's sake, a fixture of the neighborhood, practically a defining moment of New York life, and it's vanished and no one even bothered to tell you. It's sad. Not as sad

as things that are truly sad, I'll grant you that, but sad nonetheless.

Devotees of the Brooklyn Blackout cake are as passionate as Ephron was about her strudel (which happily reappeared on Second Avenue on the Upper East Side at Andre's Cafe and Bakery and, according to the internet, remains there). The earliest recorded evidence of the Brooklyn Blackout comes from a Brooklyn-based bakery named Ebinger's.

Ebinger's Brooklyn Blackout casts a long, sweet shadow that reaches into the present day. The mother of one of my best friends, now in her mid-seventies, grew up on Long Island and moved to New York City in her teens. When I casually asked if she knew of a place called Ebinger's, she said, "Of course! My great-aunt took me out to Brooklyn every year for my birthday to have a slice of cake [at Ebinger's]. It was my yearly treat." A few days later, I mentioned to this same friend's mother-in-law, a woman also in her mid-seventies, who'd grown up in Arizona but come here in her twenties after her marriage, that I was researching Ebinger's, she needed no further explanation. "Oh yes, of course," she said, matter-of-factly. "You went there for the Brooklyn Blackout."

These responses pale in comparison to the ones you

find online. There is a Facebook group dedicated to Ebinger's. There are multiple articles about Ebinger's on food blogs written in the last few years. If you search *The New York Times'* website, there are more than thirty mentions of Ebinger's from every decade from the sixties until 2017, plus a 1945 obituary for Walter Ebinger, then president of the bakery, whom the *Times* notes "was well known also as a civic leader."

Did I mention Ebinger's closed in 1972?

EBINGER'S BROOKLYN BLACKOUT STORY begins in 1898, the same year Brooklyn joined New York City. A German immigrant named George Ebinger opened a storefront on Flatbush Avenue near Cortelyou Road. Even in the nineteenth century, the Ebinger name was associated with freshness and taste. George's sons (George, Walter, and Arthur) eventually took over the business, and they expanded the business to Queens. Ebinger's signature cake was a four-layer chocolate cake, each layer separated by chocolate pudding, iced with dark chocolate fudge icing, and sprinkled with crumbs from the cake itself. Sometime during World War II, this cake acquired the name Brooklyn Blackout. So

Brooklyn Blackout Cupcake from Ladybird Bakery

christened, rumor has it, in a nod to the night blackouts Brooklyn underwent to mask the silhouettes of departing war ships from the Brooklyn Navy Yard as they sailed down the East River and out to sea.

Ebinger's striped boxes were easy to spot, and Ebinger's "girls" (the women behind the counter) were legendary. According to *The New York Times*, "the median age of the Ebinger's girls seemed to be about eighty, but they could slice and box a cake faster than women a quarter their age." When Ebinger's closed in 1972 (a victim of overexpansion; plans to move into Long Island led to bankruptcy), people reacted to it the way they responded to the Brooklyn Dodgers' move to Los Angeles. It was a tragedy. On August 27,

1972, the day after it closed, *The New York Times* noted that Ebinger's had gone "the way of the Navy Yard, the Dodgers, and Luna Park."

When word got out that Ebinger's was shuttering, people lined up to buy the last cakes and froze them, sometimes for years. One former customer highlighted in the 1991 *New York Times* article on *The Brooklyn Cookbook* said that when he finally defrosted and ate his, it "made him feel as if he were drinking his last bottle of 1929 Lafite."

That is a heck of a reputation to live up to. And many places have tried! The Brooklyn Blackout is a staple among New York bakeries, and more than a few around the country. Every once in a while a food blog will come up with its list of the best in the borough, and if you wander onto the Ebinger's Facebook group you can see the search for the "one" is still on. But few bakeries have anchored their reputation and success in it the way Ladybird has.

THIS DEVOTION TO THE Brooklyn Blackout has proven true in my own life. I cannot remember an occasion in my life, or the lives of people I care about, in which a Ladybird Blackout was not present. It's in nearly every photo of the celebrations people used to commemorate on film back when it was more expensive to develop than purchasing a large cake (also known as life before the iPhone). Do you remember the first turkey you had on Thanksgiving? The first present you opened on Christmas? For me, it's that. Such a constant presence that it blends into something you eventually take it for granted. It's always just there.

There's a repetitive shot to be found in all my pre-iPhone photo albums: one of my friends leaning over a cake to blow out candles, the angle almost always the same, the only difference being hairstyles and clothes. The cakes that were delivered to hospital rooms on the labor-and-delivery floor during visiting hours after a birth, the cupcakes left out for my goddaughter to celebrate the fact she was now a big sister, the "congratulations on graduating college at age thirty" cake, and "the loss you suffered is so huge maybe the only thing we can do is eat cake and be present for each other" cake.

Of course, what I'm talking about, what Ephron's talking about, and what the Ebinger's fanatics are talking about, is ritual. Every culture, every religion, even every city, has one.

In an early episode of *Mad Men*, first-year copywriter Peggy Olson is called upon to pitch the Popsicle account in the absence of Don Draper, the creative director. She impresses the room: "When I was little, my mother would take a Twin Pop and break it in half and give one to me and one to my sister. We were completely equal in her eyes. Beloved. . . . It has nothing to do with an ice cream truck on a hot summer day or the flavor or the color. It's a ritual. You 'Take it, break it, share it, and love it.'"

Or, in my case, buy it, slice it, dish it, and eat it.

THIS TOO IS A metaphor for the ritual of Ladybird itself, and arguably all bakeries and baked goods that last long enough to play a role in the lives of their customers. Every city has its own food item it's especially faithful to. In New Orleans there's the beignet; in France bread is practically considered a civil right. After the terrorist attacks in November 2015, Parisians were confined to their homes, except to acquire their daily baguette. In New York there are dozens of items associated with the city: local food blogs never tire of publishing lists of the city's best pizzas or bagels. But the fame of these items come second to what they signify: a sense of celebration and continuity (for what is celebration, really, but a way to measure our own progress) in our lives. It matters less what they are, than that they are present. And perhaps no institution that's not religious is so intertwined with celebration, large and small, than the bakery.

It's a role Clemens takes very seriously. She can remember cakes she's made decades ago. When a cake goes out for someone's birthday, she knows who the person is because she likely decorated the one that went out the previous year. "It should be a nice cake. I don't want to screw up their birthday."

The customers come from all over. She waves her arm toward the window. "We get them from Brooklyn, from Queens, from Long Island, from Staten Island, even." If they've ever lived in the neighborhood and come back for any reason, they stop by. If they've ever worked in the neighborhood—in the hospital, or doing construction, or even at the events at Prospect Park in the summer—"They make a point of coming back." She's baked birthday cakes for customers when they were teenagers, gone on to bake their wedding cakes, and is now baking cakes for their baby showers. Two of the people who work behind the counter came here after school as children.

"It's generations," she says of how Ladybird has influenced the neighborhood.

5

BECOMING A BAKER

When Clemens opened Ladybird in 1994, it was, to borrow the phrase, a different world. Real estate, for one, was significantly less expensive, shockingly so in many neighborhoods, even when accounting for inflation. For another, there was no internet, no social media, no crowdfunding. Yet the process of opening a brick-and-mortar bakery these days remains surprisingly similar for entrepreneurs despite all the changes the world has seen.

The truth about bakers, particularly those who opt to open their own business, is that they are rarely motivated by the money. Baking is a vocation, a way of life—quite a specific one, at that—and the people who pursue it are often driven by the desire to create and share something as much as writers are compelled to write, or doctors to save lives.

When Nicole Cramer, owner of My Grandma Baked a

Cookie, decided to reorient her life toward baking—and away from a successful fifteen-year-long career in global advertising—her primary motivation was the desire to keep alive the recipes and traditions of her grandmother.

Cramer grew up in midtown Manhattan but spent weekends, holidays, and entire summers with her grandmother Ruth in central Pennsylvania. Ruth had been born into a Mennonite family in central Pennsylvania in 1926. The youngest of eight children, six of whom survived, by the age of thirteen she'd taken on the cooking and baking responsibilities for her family, including the men who worked on the farm. One of Cramer's first memories is being three years old and attached to Ruth's apron, surrounded by the smells of the kitchen.

"She taught me that baking was a necessity," says Cramer, "but also a point of joy and a point of sharing. You never went to her house without, first of all, a warm welcome. There was no, 'Oh, who's at the door?' It was always, 'Somebody's knocking at the door? Invite them in.'" Cramer recalls that Ruth would always yell a welcome in Pennsylvania Dutch, "There's a connotation to the word, like come in, sit down, eat. It's not all said, but it's all understood. If you accept an invitation in, you're going to be fed,

Nicole Cramer, owner of My Grandma Baked a Cookie

and you're going to be staying longer than you expected, so just get used to it."

When Cramer was old enough to have her own kitchen, baking became an escape from her high-stress career in the city. "I would come home, I would turn on jazz, get in the kitchen, create something."

After Ruth passed away in 2012, it was not just her absence that was so difficult to come to terms with but all the baking that had gone with her. At Ruth's memorial service, the family provided an open mic so that attendees could share what they had loved most about Ruth and what they would miss the most. Every person who stood to speak—

"literally every single person," says Cramer—began by mentioning something Ruth had baked. From this experience, Cramer began to think of ways in which she could extend her grandmother's baking legacy.

"She was all about cooking and conversation. You came in, you ate, you shared, and whether you intended to spend three minutes, you spent three hours, and you felt better about yourself and you felt nourished physically and emotionally when you left her home."

It's a legacy, Cramer thinks, that would have surprised her grandmother.

"She never sold a baked good in her life, she never thought 'Oh, I want people to feel warm when they come to her house,' that was just her. I was like, 'How can I re-create that and give her this larger legacy and take it to a larger community?' Because she never left. She got married and lived eight miles from where she was born. That was the circumference of her life. People within a fifty-mile radius kind of knew her, but beyond that, she never traveled, she never got on an airplane, any of those things. I just wanted to bring her spirit to a larger community, and build a community around what she would've done had she had this business."

Cramer started small in 2013. She'd bake enough cookies to fill a basket and then bring them into her job and put them on her desk where coworkers could come by and purchase a package "or ten" says Cramer, laughing. Within a year, she began baking cookies for work events, but continued to place the basket on her desk that was now filled with leftovers from organized functions. "I was like the Pied Piper; people followed me from the elevator to my desk and wait until I got out my little credit card–swipe thing for my phone, and they would buy cookies."

It was this level of devotion, and the way it resembled both Cramer's and her grandmother's passion for baking, that pushed her to the next level. "I remember thinking, 'Wait a second, I need to actually make this a bigger thing, because how much love am I giving my grandmother by selling cookies from my desk?'"

In 2016, Cramer left advertising, and turned her full attention to My Grandma Baked a Cookie, which opened its first location in 2017. Or almost her full attention. In order to fund the enterprise and also continue to pay her own bills, Cramer kept the part-time consulting business she'd been running on the side for the past two decades. Called NicNic Productions, the business focuses on helping women entrepreneurs, small-business owners, and executives produce their best brands, best businesses, and best selves. Cramer was about to experience the other side of that world.

Making the leap from a successful career in advertising to owning a bakery sounds extreme, but in fact Cramer's life had long been defined by a variety of seemingly incompatible activities and professions. Growing up, she'd been a child actor, appearing on *Sesame Street* and various musical theater productions from the age of five all the way to college. She plays five instruments and is a professionally trained soprano. At Cornell University, she enrolled in a pre-vet animal science program; at one point, she taught dance. Still, when she decided to leave her full-time job and throw her energy behind baking, it involved a lot of the sort of trial and error that is often the result of deciding to mix a passion project with the realities of commerce. To begin with, she was determined to make sure her product remained connected to Ruth in the most direct way possible: by cooking everything *literally* in her grandmother's kitchen. This is an endearing anecdote—and a helpful branding exercise—but in reality it meant that Cramer was often driving to the house in Pennsylvania, three and a half hours from New York, baking overnight, and then driving back to the city. "It was a stupid way to do a business," she now concedes, "but I'm a little bit of a masochistic worka-holic, so it made sense for me."

She also opted to open her first brick-and-mortar store in Pennsylvania, near her grandmother's home, in an effort to stay true to her Pennsylvania Dutch origins, instead of in an urban center. So much of Cramer's career in advertising had been focusing on brand work that she felt she couldn't now step away from that training.

"I felt like I couldn't be off-brand and look for a place in New York or somewhere else when I'm honoring my Penn-sylvania Dutch grandmother. I should have gotten over my-self in that regard. I should've gone where I knew I had the audience. And my audience, because of my network and my background, was in New York. I probably should've just bit the bullet, figured out how to find even the tiniest base that I could manage, and started there."

Instead, Cramer launched My Grandma Baked a Cookie's first location in a strip mall on Route 940 deep in the Poconos. The phrase "strip mall" does not necessarily conjure up visions of old-fashioned hominess, but the atmo-sphere, or the "experience" as Cramer calls it, once people walk through the door lives up to Ruth's legacy. "Everybody comments that they weren't expecting the place to be so cute. It also always smells delicious; it always feels like Grandma herself was there. She has a little chair in the corner actually with GRANDMA RUTH written on it, that's kind of our homage to her. And you get a warm welcome. You get our version of her yelling out her kitchen door."

Cramer estimates her opening budget ran her about $150,000. This number accounts for the renovation of a rental space that was previously a "pastry shop" but did not have a kitchen. It also covered baking equipment, including ovens, refrigerators, workbenches, built-in storage, sinks, commercial flooring, upgraded electrical wiring, and more. Additionally, Cramer had to outfit the rest of the café, including the storage room and office, and pay for insurance. She also needed to ensure she could fund payroll during six weeks of training and recipe testing, as well as the first six months of operation. Finally, she needed to remind the community that the bakery was actually there and worth frequenting, something she says many new businesses don't budget for.

"I find that so many start-ups forget about costs associated with items like signage. Not just main signs but OPEN flags, sales, COMING SOON banners, packaging—there are so many packaging items associated with baking—and office supplies. Bakeries still need tape, paper clips, printer cartridges, PAID stamps."

Cramer was fortunate, however, that there were a few big-ticket items she didn't have to purchase, including a number of café table-and-chair sets and two pastry cases.

The other challenge facing a bakery that is not true of another small-business start-up is that its products are good for about twenty-four hours. (Alas for the days of liquor-soaked and sugar-filled Victorian cakes that would last months!) All business owners operate with a certain combination of adventure and faith, but Cramer believes it requires a level of insanity to get into the perishable-food game. It is the "extreme level of 'What the hell was I thinking here?'" she says, comparing her endeavor to friends who have ice cream businesses, with products that can stay in freezers for weeks. "I literally bake a loaf of bread and by the end of the day it's done, it's dead. When people ask you, 'How many hours old is this?' You're like, 'I'm sorry. It's not a baby. What do you mean? It's delicious. Eat it.'"

When the shop first opened, Cramer was the sole baker, doing everything by hand—*her* hand. Which is ironic considering she "actually got into this to own a bakery, not to become a baker." But she quickly discovered that unless one has the financial means to bankroll an entire operation, including the hiring of chefs, "you better be the baker, or know how to be, at least in that first year, two years, whatever it might be." As anyone in the food service industry can tell you, the margin on food is very small and leaves little room for salaries, especially during the heavy financial lifting at the beginning when one has to invest not only in the space and supplies but also in the build-out and equipment. Even though Cramer was accustomed to putting in eighteen-hour days, and expected similar now, the physicality of baking took her off guard. "I went from sitting and running around but mostly sitting in meetings to always, relentlessly being on my feet for hours on end, except for that fifteen minutes where I sit down and suck down a cup of coffee and pray."

The menu she currently serves is a combination of Ruth's recipes combined with her great-grandmother's recipes, as well as recipes she's adapted from the community cookbooks of local Mennonites she's collected over the decades.

She's also added in a few of her own creations: "They're things that I've created out of my own love of travel, being a New Yorker. It's a combination of Pennsylvania Dutch and a person who's been to eighty-six countries."

Starting out, one advantage of being the sole baker was that Cramer didn't have to worry much about the fact that she hadn't been professionally trained. She'd learned everything from Ruth, including how things should *feel* versus how to measure specifically for certain recipes. "We are meticulous about certain things, but sometimes you're just like . . . you have to know what it feels like." It's only now that the bakery has been up and running for a few years that Cramer and her head baker, who operates in a similar way, are focusing on figuring out how to measure things accurately so that they can teach the next generation of bakers they are hiring.

WHEN JESSE SCHUMANN BEGAN the long road to open Sea Wolf bakery in Seattle, he had very little sense that he was pursuing a career in baking. He was in his early twenties and still trying to sort out what he wanted to do with his life—without much success. "I was a pretty terrible employee," he concedes in hindsight. "I was really surprised at how much I didn't like working in an office. I had a pretty bad attitude, and I got fired from a number of jobs." Three years of what he terms "real jobs" made it clear to Jesse that he needed to find a different kind of environment to work in, and he began halfheartedly casting about for training for a vocation. "I imagined upholstery or woodworking, some of the standard romanticized things, but I never did anything to move forward on that." Instead he remained at his low-level job in Oregon politics, but allowed a friend who managed a local bakery to connect him with the baker there. Soon he was filling in on weekends.

"Thinking back, it was one of the sweetest, easiest baking jobs ever. We worked in the old district, the Pearl, and it was this big brick building. It was old, kind of industrial chic. And he would mix some dough in this tall ceiling brick room, go have a cigarette outside in the sun, and sit on the stoop and drink some coffee. Then he'd go back in, bake some stuff, go have another cigarette."

Jesse enjoyed his time in the bakery enough that, when he was eventually fired from his politics job, he decided to seek out additional training. "I found the San Francisco

Baking Institute had a professional program that was nine months part-time so you could work. It was great."

The San Francisco Baking Institute was founded in 1996 by Frenchman Michel Saus, a former pastry chef at the Michelin-starred Barrier restaurant in Tours, France, and his wife, Evelyne Saus. It is currently the only school in the United States dedicated to artisan baking. It no longer offers the full-time (eighteen weeks) or part-time (twenty-four weeks) Bread and Pastry Professional Training Program that Jesse took, but still provides a variety of five-day and weekend bread and pastry classes, costing between $400 to $1100, aimed at both amateur and professional bakers.

"I had a great time," Jesse recalls. "There were wonderful teachers that I still really respect and try to keep in touch with professionally. And I left it just really excited about baking and really prideful and convinced that I knew all the best techniques and stuff like that."

Jesse's experience highlights one of the advantages of formalized instruction: on-the-ground training to learn and practice procedures, in a professional setting using professional tools, with the added benefit of lasting connections who can provide recommendations as well as support. When Clemens left CIA, for instance, it was the school's alum network that provided her with jobs during her first few years as a working baker.

IRONICALLY, THE EXPLOSION OF interest in cooking and baking both as a pastime and source of entertainment has not resulted in an increase of culinary school enrollment. In fact, many culinary schools have been streamlining their classes or shutting down altogether in recent years. In 2017, the famous Le Cordon Bleu school closed all its US locations. One of the primary challenges these schools face is the rising cost of tuition versus the relatively low starting salaries of restaurant jobs. Financial aid can also be tough to get. There is also the fact that those interested in careers in the culinary world often have the option of getting on-the-job experience without formal training. Even so, people who prefer classes still have plenty of options. Schools like CIA and the Institute of Culinary Education (ICE) offer a wide variety of programs that cover the culinary arts, pastry arts, bread baking, cake techniques, and sommelier training. Some, like the International Culinary Center, offer more specific classes like farm-to-table culinary and Italian culinary. Increasingly, schools provide programs in hospitality management and instruction of the business side of the industry.

Programs offering associate degrees run two years, and many schools stipulate a certain amount of "real world" hours performed before a degree is granted. For instance, the New England Culinary Institute (NECI) requires between 135 to 495 hours of externship, depending on the degree level. The advantages of these schools, particularly for those with an interest in culinary arts but with little experience or connections, is that they offer comprehensive training and a network of connections that can be beneficial for many years to come. But, again, it doesn't come cheap. ICE's pastry and baking arts program, which offers eight-, ten-, and twelve-month options, costs $29,900 to $39,900.

The cost per semester at CIA for the Associate and Bachelor's Degree Programs is $17,710.

JESSE GRADUATED IN THE fall of 2009 and opted to return to Portland. He then followed a similar route to Clemens, working at smaller bakeries around the city to try new things and hone his craft, including a year at Little T Baker on Division Street, which had opened in 2008 and quickly became a contender for the best bread in Portland. He was still at Little T when a friend from the San Francisco Baking Institute called to say he was opening a bakery in Wisconsin and asked if Jesse wanted to come and help him open.

Jesse decided to go. The experience offered him a front-row seat to realities of starting a new business. "That was a really educational experience. I learned a lot about the pitfalls of opening a business and how not to overextend yourself." In the fall of 2012, he returned to the Pacific Northwest with high hopes. "I was turning thirty and I thought everything was going to change, everything was going to happen, and I was going to hit my stride and do my thing." Alas, reality proved somewhat different: "I proceeded to have a pretty miserable couple of years. Just ups and downs. But during that time, I worked at the Breadfarm."

Founded in 2003, Breadfarm is an artisan bakery located just shy of seventy-four miles north of Seattle, in a tiny village called Edison on the shores of Bellingham Bay. The bakery specializes in hand-crafted goods and naturally leavens its breads using wild yeasts.

Jesse describes his time at Breadfarm as "really delightful" and remains close with owners Scott Mangold and Renée Bourgault. During this time, Jesse's brother Kit was following a similar path; he'd worked at Breadfarm, too, and then enrolled in Seattle Central's culinary program, which at the time was a two-year program that, in addition to teaching all of the normal culinary skills, also offered a side focus on bread and pastries.

While Jesse was moving between jobs, Kit was tapped to help open The Whale Wins, Renee Erickson's third restaurant in Seattle. Erickson is a James Beard Award–winning chef who owns restaurants, bars, and a small chain of doughnut shops in Seattle. Eventually the Schumanns began baking bread for Erickson's restaurants—"Renee has the reputation of supporting her employees as they went off on their various independent ventures"—that led to her leasing them a space in her first restaurant, the Boat Street Café.

"So, we would go in there at midnight as they were closing up, and we would have premixed our dough by hand and would carry it in bus tubs. And we had bought a bunch of cast-iron pans to follow the Jim Lahey baking method where you bake in a Dutch oven that mimics the environment of a professional oven." Lahey is the founder of the Sullivan Street Bakery in New York City. A former sculptor, he opened the bakery in 1994 after failing to find any bread in the city that resembled the crusty sort he'd eaten while living in Italy. He later made famous "no-knead bread," which, as its name suggests, requires no kneading, special ingredients, nor equipment. *The New York Times* calls it "one of the most popular recipes" it's ever published. Says Jesse, "You can get really nice, professional-quality bread in that way. So we bought eight of these pans. And from midnight to eight a.m. we would shape and proof and bake these loaves eight at a time."

Eventually, the bread became so successful that after two years of this taxing night schedule the Schumanns were able to move into their own space. And with that, Sea Wolf was created.

"It was entirely bootstrapped," says Jesse, who estimates the opening costs to be about $500,000 split evenly between build-out and equipment purchase. "The only investors were our parents, who helped us buy the first eight pans. We got a loan and got a lease, and the big piece for the loan, our folks took out, put up their little rental house as equity for the loan. Because money was the big missing piece.

"We did it this way because we didn't have any money. We didn't have any business acumen. In hindsight it was very difficult, very tiring, very stressful. But it was a great way to slowly learn what the hell we were doing, to grow

Croissants from Sea Wolf Bakery

a customer base. And unbeknownst to us at this point we were also, I think, growing what would eventually become our regional base."

Sea Wolf is a light and airy space, located between the Wallingford and Fremont neighborhoods of Seattle, and has become a community staple. Beyond the physical storefront, Sea Wolf also sells bread at three farmers markets year-round, with an additional six locations in the summer, and to almost twenty restaurants in Seattle.

Looking ahead, Jesse would like to expand Sea Wolf into another location. "Right now our first priority is to get into a second space that will serve as retail and be our pastry production spot. We do a lot of croissants, and we do a lot of bread. If we can split those two out, then everyone has more elbow room and we have the advantage of a second retail space that can catch some overflow. At the moment, I worry about the weekends. During the busy times I worry that people's experiences are less in quality. So, if we had a second spot where we could take on some of that, I'd feel better for our employees and for our customers."

While challenging, a second location would no doubt benefit not only from all the lessons the Schumanns learned getting Sea Wolf off the ground but also from all their connections. The baking world is surprisingly small and interconnected. Without question, part of Sea Wolf's success was due to the brothers' having established contacts in the industry and being able to lean on them for both hard-won knowledge as well as financial support.

"We had the advantage of being in these wonderful relatively high-profile restaurants like The Whale [Wins] and The Walrus and Carpenter," says Jesse. "So people had been eating our bread for a couple years that they couldn't get anywhere else."

It's something Jesse hopes to pay forward.

"We've built Sea Wolf in an old-fashioned way. I've been

really proud of the people that work for us. We have the nicest . . . happiest environment I've ever worked in. And that is a credit to the people that have approached us to come work for us. And I want to make it the same way that you practice baking, refine your baking. I want to refine the business—make it better and better and better."

6

A.D. *SATC*

July 9, 2000, is a date that will live in infamy in the cupcake world. It is the airdate of season three, episode
five of HBO's smash hit *Sex and the City* (*SATC*). It can be
difficult to remember in a time when television shows are
designed to be streamed and binged, but prior to *Sex and
the City*'s premiere in 1998 HBO's original productions
were almost all sports. After its premiere, the show increasingly captured the imagination of an entire country with
its glamorous, shockingly honest depictions of four single
women's lives in New York City; bars began devoting entire
nights to watch parties, crowds gathered everywhere it was
filming, and the front page of the *New York Post* reported on
minor plot developments. By its third season, the series had
an obsessive audience (both national and international) por-
ing over its every word and featured outfit. No detail was
overlooked. This audience provided an intense gaze when

nine minutes and eighteen seconds into the episode "No Ifs, Ands, or Butts" (yes, the extra *t* is intentional) Carrie Bradshaw declares, "I have a crush." That crush is Aidan, soon to be the anti-Big (Carrie's ex) romantic dating ideal of a generation of women, but at this point he was just a scruffy furniture dude whom Carrie's gay best friend spotted in a *New York Times* style feature.

"I have a crush," says Carrie.

Carrie and Miranda are sitting on a bench in front of a café somewhere in Greenwich Village. The camera pans out to show that the awning above their heads reads THE MAGNOLIA BAKERY. A car drives by the storefront. The shot lasts one second. Then we are back with Carrie and Miranda on the bench. Carrie is peeling away the paper wrapper around the bottom of her yellow cupcake with pink icing. Miranda remarks that Carrie hasn't had a crush in a while, "not since Big." "Big wasn't a crush, he was a crash," says Carrie dryly before taking an enormous bite out of the cupcake, icing and all. The conversation about crushes continues, a cupcake bite punctuating each back and forth. Crumbs fall off Carrie's lips.

If you were to calculate the number of cupcakes subsequently sold based on the one second that Magnolia

Bakery's name appears on-screen, it might turn out to be the most valuable one second of screen time any company has ever inadvertently found its way into. Or intentionally, for that matter! No multimillion-dollar Super Bowl ad has ever been this effective. Even the Manolo Blahniks Carrie was so famous for wearing could not claim to have benefited quite this much from so little. Of course, four-hundred-dollar shoes are less accessible to the regular viewer (particularly the twentysomething audience who viewed *Sex and the City* as an aspirational guide to life) than a three-dollar cupcake. And the price point was surely one of the things that made those cupcakes so appealing.

This was not the first time a fictional story set in New York City started a particular food craze. Some will no doubt recall "The Soup Nazi" episode of *Seinfeld* that made famous the real-life soup vendor Ali Yeganeh or even the notable scene from *When Harry Met Sally* . . . that put both pastrami sandwiches and Katz's Delicatessen on the map. It was not even the first time *Sex and the City* had launched an, if not exactly food, imbibing craze: When I waited tables in Greenwich Village around this time, my colleagues and I suddenly found ourselves inundated with requests for cosmopolitans, Carrie's signature drink.

Needless to say, you can get a cosmo at any bar with vodka and cranberry juice in stock and neither soup nor pastrami are all that sexy. But what *Sex and the City* did with its one-second shot was provide an easy way for women looking to emulate Carrie's life to do so in an inexpensive and aspirational way. And who could blame them? It appeared to be a great life. For women raised to think enjoying decadent food was only slightly less criminal than committing murder, it was gratifying, if not slightly rebellious, to watch a beautiful woman eat an enormous sweet.

Magnolia Bakery was only a few years old when it experienced its one second (and then many decades) of fame. It was opened in 1996 at the corner of Bleecker and West Eleventh Streets, the heart of the West Village, by friends Jennifer Appel and Allysa Torey. Much like the origin story of the British Cadbury Flake bar (which, legend has it, was simply created as a way to use up the leftover chocolate flakes from other confections), the Magnolia cupcake came about when the partners found themselves with extra cake batter and decided to put it to use instead of letting it go to waste. "One minute we were making eight cupcakes. The next minute we had windows full of them," Torey told *New York* magazine's Adam Sternberg back in 2005.

Not long after the episode aired, and then for a long time after, pilgrimages to Magnolia Bakery became an essential part of visits to New York City. 'Round-the-block lines were the norm. Tour buses started navigating the narrow streets of Greenwich Village to stop in front of the bakery. In his compelling book, *Vanishing New York: How a Great City Lost Its Soul*, Jeremiah Moss pinpoints this moment when things changed for New York. And, he argues, not for the better. In fact, he uses such vehement language one might wonder whether the Magnolia cupcake is some latter-day Stay Puft Marshmallow Man, stomping through the city, destroying everything in its path. Similarly, in David Rakoff's 2010 book *Half Empty*, he writes: "A metropolis of streets once thriving with local businesses and services now consisting of nothing but Marc Jacobs store after Marc Jacobs store and cupcake purveyors (is there anything more blandly sweet, less evocative of this great city, and more *goyish* than any other baked good with the possible exception of Eucharist wafers than the cupcake?)."

He wasn't the only one who found the explosion of cupcakes (cupcakes!) controversial. Ruth Reichl, then editor in chief of Condé Nast's venerable *Gourmet* magazine, put cupcakes on the cover of the January 2004 issue. It wasn't actually even just cupcakes, it was a cake *decorated* with cupcakes on top, the idea being children could pluck them off and parents would be left with the cake to eat. She was inundated with hate mail from readers for months afterward, filled with accusations that she was lowering the standard of the magazine by featuring such common fare. She later told an interviewer: "It finally hit me that we had unwittingly sent a message to the readers. That what we were saying to the readers of what had once been a very elite group of people— the gourmands, the gourmets of the world who thought that the world of fine food belong to them—and for them, cupcakes were children's food or plebeian food . . . And what we were saying is: You do not own this anymore. That food has become much bigger than your little, gourmet world."

But for the cupcake industry all this controversy was a boon. Or perhaps it's more accurate to say it was from these few seconds that the cupcake industry as we know it was born. Says Jessica Reed, "*Sex and the City* and Magnolia Bakery are a jumping-off point of the cupcake craze." There had been cupcakes before, obviously, but like *Frasier*'s coffee bar, they now became a *thing*, a lifestyle unto themselves. Extravagantly decorated, overpriced, and everywhere. Magnolia Bakery even took a star turn in a 2005

Saturday Night Live digital short titled "Lazy Sunday" in which Andy Samberg and Chris Parnell ate its cupcakes before seeing a film. The video went viral. Cupcakes began replacing traditional cakes at weddings, and they became an acceptable part of daily life, not just a "sometimes treat" and not just for children.

What's important about this story from a business standpoint is that cupcakes quite suddenly became a viable business option. In 2003 Crumbs opened a gourmet cupcake chain, selling a dozen one-inch "taste pack" of cupcakes for $24 and a "colossal" cupcake that could serve up to eight people for $42; it grew to seventy-nine locations in nine states by 2013. In 2009 Baked by Melissa opened, offering a wide array of mini cupcakes. In 2012 cupcake ATMs began popping up, filled with sweets from Sprinkles. At least for a while, baking cupcakes became a hobby a person could choose to do as a full-time career. Until it wasn't. The cupcake craze would end circa 2014, when Crumbs, once the darling of Wall Street, declared bankruptcy. As it turned out, it is tough to run a successful business based on low-priced (at least in the grand scheme of things), perishable items. By this point, however, we lived in a different world when it came to baked goods. Whether cupcakes alone could sustain the bottom line, their enormous impact changed the way we regarded and consumed desserts. They were the gateway into even more decadent, extravagantly decorated goods. This was what Clemens had been waiting for. Cake decorating had been her first love, and there was now a market for it.

CLEMENS IS KEEN TO point out that she has never followed a craze. Not the cupcake craze ("I would never create a whole bakery based on cupcakes. I tell everybody, 'You can sell a hundred cupcakes and you're going to get the same amount of money as you do for one big cake.'"), the gluten-free craze, nor the whole-grain craze, which may account for at least part of her success. "I never have tried to do any of the bandwagons. I really pretty much stay true to what works for me," she says.

But even though she doesn't think she's ever even seen the "cupcake" episode of *Sex and the City*, she remembers the moment clearly and is quick to acknowledge its effect on her business.

"It changed everything," she says.

Before that, most people came in to purchase simple cakes, "more like a home style." Breakfast was the bakery's busiest time—scones and muffins and biscuits. "We would never sell a cake at the beginning of the week, and now we sell cakes all week long because people take them to the office." What shifted was arguably not only the emergence of cupcakes as their own economy but also people's understanding of what cakes *could*, and possibly *should*, be and the role they played in everyday lives.

"Cakes and cupcakes became more of this kind of sexy, indulgent thing," says Clemens. "It became more of a mainstream thing with younger people. Eventually the millennials started taking pictures of it and like, 'I'm getting this' or 'I'm treating myself to this cupcake.' It all kind of came together in time."

By the time the cupcake craze hit, Clemens and Winkler had spent a few years retooling their inherited Blackout recipe from Faith (the recipe remains a secret, though it was hinted to me that the fact I love the cake and feel similarly about coffee was not a coincidence) and had reintroduced it along with a few other, full-size cakes. With cakes on the menu, and a clientele who was increasingly open to the idea of highly decorated baked goods as an everyday thing, Clemens was also able to indulge in the thing she loved most: flowers.

Decorated Cakes from Ladybird Bakery

"I like making flowers. I just I really do. I really love making flowers. I like how they change seasonally. For instance, we started going the all-pink route this past weekend and we'll go into that for a while. And by the time I get tired of that we'll go to St. Patrick's, and then it's just seasonal."

This is my original impression of Two Little Red Hens, as it was called when I first arrived as a customer (and pictures from my old photo albums back me up): the extravagant flowers atop the cakes in the case. As if a bouquet was bursting from the cake itself. "Oh yes," says Clemens when I attempt to describe one particular cake that stands out in my memory, which I purchased approximately fifteen years ago. "You mean the dragonfly cake. And the wings were made out of almonds." I had forgotten the wings, but yes!

"I came up with that one," says Clemens with a knowing smile.

At the risk of sounding like a *Sex and the City* voice-over, things were blooming in Clemens's personal life around this time as well. Sometime after she and Winkler opened up on Eighth Avenue, a young man who lived across the street began to make regular appearances at the bakery.

"He would buy banana bread and he would give it to his cat and then he'd come back over for more. Then in the evenings I'd pull down the gates really hard and I'd look up to see if he was looking down, and finally . . . It was truly very much a romantic tale." So romantic that Clemens gave up her rent-controlled apartment to live with him. They've been together ever since and now have two children.

Meanwhile, by the end of 2000, things were going so well that Clemens and Winkler decided it was time to open a second location. By 2001, they signed a lease for a space on Second Avenue on the Upper East Side, but the reality of the commute between the two locations became less and less appealing to Clemens. She explains, "I was pregnant, I had a little one, I was only going there a couple times a week. I was commuting and I was nursing. I hated it. I absolutely hated it. And I just wanted to be here. I didn't want to be bigger. It wasn't working. And my husband said, 'Why don't you take Brooklyn and she takes Manhattan?'"

Which is precisely what happened. As part of the agreement, Clemens kept the store in Brooklyn and Winkler kept the name and moved to the Upper East Side location. I relay to Clemens the rumor I'd always heard that one partner kept the name and the other kept the Blackout recipe, which is a measure of what Brooklyn regulars prioritized. Clemens laughs at this, and reassures me both bakeries still sell the same Blackout. I also recall the sign that went up at the cash register right around this time asking for new name suggestions. How did Clemens land on Ladybird?

It goes back to Texas, and to her beloved flowers.

"I ran a contest and I asked everybody to help and I got a lot of names, and I was leaning toward Bluebird, Bluebell, Bluebonnet—I really liked Bluebonnet 'cause I'm from Texas, but if I said it they'll think we're like margarine." She already knew she wanted the logo to be wildflowers, so when her friend suggested the name *Ladybird*, that was it. It "all kind of clicked together."

Clemens also saw it as a reference to "Lady Bird" Johnson, a fellow Texan who was the First Lady during Clemens's youth. "She did so much for this country that she doesn't really get credit for. She planted wildflower seeds that are still blooming. She was really one of the first environmentalists. It was about beautification of the highways, but it was all over the country. She went and cultivated these wildflowers, some nearly extinct, and scattered the seeds all over the highways all over the country, and we have her to thank for that."

7

I DON'T SMELL ANYTHING

Baking a cake is a multiday process. Even the freshest cakes begin their path to the display case anywhere between thirty-six to forty-eight hours prior to their arrival there. This, as much as anything, accounts for Ladybird's requirement that customers make their orders forty-eight to seventy-two hours in advance. It's also an acknowledgment that orchestrating the time line of a bakery schedule, like so much else about baking, often feels like a great math equation. Carrying out that time line, meanwhile, feels a lot like a relay race. One person bakes the cakes on Monday. Another fills them on Tuesday. Yet another frosts them on Wednesday. This order is particularly important when it comes to the Blackout cake since it's filled with a rich, chocolate pudding that needs time to cool and set or it won't hold between the layers.

Ladybird's biggest seller by far is the Brooklyn Blackout cake; it accounts for one-third of all of cake sales. It may be special guest star at my and others' special functions, but here it is the workhorse. It's what pays the rent. Inevitably that familiarity, the pure number of Blackouts the bakery has to produce each day, has bred an aversion among the Ladybird staff. Hardly anyone at Ladybird eats the Blackout—it's simply too much. Too much chocolate. Too much sugar. Too much richness. *Too much*, too much.

Vicky, the college student who works behind the counter, says the first time she tried the Blackout cupcake she scraped the thick layer of icing off the top and merely ate the cake and pudding—and even that took her two days. Her coworker Shyran discloses that she routinely tells customers the cupcake—which measures approximately three inches by three inches, iced—is so intense it can easily serve two to three people. Clemens herself has long sworn off the chocolate—"I haven't had a Blackout in years."

Every employee, of course, has the menu item they love the most, which sometimes comes down to merely being the baked good one becomes the least tired of eating day after day. No one has tired of breakfast scones, for instance (including the customers; the scones often sell out before 10:00 a.m.). Anyone who's worked with food is familiar with this particular dance of too much of a good thing. It's also the challenge of turning something you love into a business: Do you love it enough to still love it all day every day? How do you keep the romance alive, so to speak? The answer is, as often as it is not, abstinence.

Shyran, for instance, prefers the Carrot cake, which unlike most carrot cakes does not contain walnuts. Clemens still has a taste for the pastry filling that is used to fill a number of the other cakes. The other night she says she took a bowl of it home and dipped pita chips in it; the sweet tooth's version of guacamole and tortilla chips. And in fact, no one who works in the back eats the cakes at all. When Roman wants something sweet he makes his family a pineapple upside-down cake from a recipe passed down in his family; the only Ladybird cakes he tastes these days are the ones introduced seasonally, and in those cases it's a quality check to make sure the recipe and results remain unchanged. But perhaps no one has sworn off the Blackouts quite as vehemently as the man who is in charge of filling and frosting them.

EDGAR ARRIVES AT LADYBIRD around 8:00 a.m. He's running late today because his six-month-old daughter,

Abigail, is sick. He also has a two-year-old son, and both are home with his wife. Edgar is younger than Roman and Pedro and sports a small goatee. He's been working here since he was a teenager—more than fifteen years. Like Roman, he commutes every morning from a different part of Brooklyn; in his case East New York, a neighborhood that's farther out than Ditmas Park, closer to JFK airport. In the warmer months, he rides his bike—it's about a forty-five-minute bike ride—but on this cold March morning, he's taken the train.

Edgar works from the baking station downstairs, which gives him access to the walk-in fridge to his right, allowing him to swiftly remove the cakes when it's time for them to be frosted or filled. The wall above his station is decorated with a plastic-covered poster that depicts a man on horseback wearing a sombrero and a kneeling young woman with a scarf over her head, holding flowers. In front of them is Jesus on the cross. To the right of the poster is a framed picture of Edgar's son, Edgar Jr., and to the right of that, another of Edgar holding his daughter. His iPhone is connected to a small, portable stereo, and he's streaming pregame coverage of a big soccer game taking place later today between Club América and Guadalajara. I ask him which team he's rooting for. "América," he replies. "The better team."

Edgar has an especially long day ahead. First, he has to fill and frost all the cakes that will be sold from the case; this list includes the Yellow cakes that are filled with pastry cream or jam, as well as the Blackouts that are filled with pudding and topped with fudge. In the early afternoon, he will frost all the special orders. If all goes according to plan, by mid-afternoon he'll turn his attention to frosting all the Blackouts required for the weekend.

Each day when he comes in, he looks at the display case to get a sense of what has sold. The case ebbs and flows like the tide. At the beginning of the week it's at its emptiest, as the days go by different parts begin to fill up; first tarts, which have the longest shelf life, then pies, next cakes, until the end of the week it's packed with baked goods. Everyone in the kitchen has worked here so long that their feeling for numbers is instinctual; like farmers who can sense a change in the weather, they don't need to be told when something is overstocked or that customers will begin asking for a particular item in the near future. In fact, weather often *is* the factor: according to Clemens, "The second the weather changes people will stop wanting mousse and want something else."

Weather sometimes affects people's buying habits in more concrete ways. "One year there was an ice storm on Valentine's. That was a bad year. So now I'm always very cautious about Valentine's. We'll only do special goods, if the weather looks good. I *always* look at the weather."

And then there's the reverse, where baked goods behave as their own sort of barometer. A few days ago, Clemens told me we'd be in a recession by September. "I'm sure of it. I've been through two of them." When people are feeling financially secure, she says they always pick up extra baked goods. When they're less sure, they get the "one pie they ordered, and that's it." Lately people have been picking up only the item ordered. "Ask any small-business person, and they can tell you right away."

In the beginning, Clemens was sometimes burned badly by not being able to intuit these critical signs, often finding herself left with too much of one item at the end of the day. Ladybird's cakes can be sold for only a day or two after they go into the case, and to be left with an abundance of unsalvageable merchandise can make or break a small business. It didn't take long before Clemens changed her ways, preferring to run the risk she might run out of product rather than overstock. "Now when I open for a holiday like Thanksgiving I have things ninety percent sold before we open the door. This was something I learned after many years. I'll set my number: We're going to make a hundred apple pies. And after that we cut off the orders. Maybe we'll have seventy-five orders, in which case I know I have twenty-five extra. When that happens, I'll tell people in the days leading up, 'If you pay now you can come and get your apple pie.' It means I may not have one apple pie extra to sell, but that's fine with me, because I don't want to be stuck with stuff." In other words, Clemens is willing to risk some unhappy walk-in customers who may not have planned ahead in order to ensure the bakery stays in safe financial waters.

"You want to come out of holiday being pretty much sold out," says Clemens, "because the week after [the] holiday, you're dead."

This is especially true during years when Easter and Passover overlap. In New York, many people celebrate both and they often coincide with spring break, meaning the week after the holidays is an especially dead time in the bakery. "It can throw a whole wrench in business," says Clemens, who has already looked up what day Passover begins next year: "It's on a Wednesday."

And then there are the holidays that can't be gamed successfully. The time around Independence Day is so dead that Clemens closes the bakery entirely for two weeks, using the time to catch up on any repairs the bakery might need. This year it will be getting a new table that Clemens hopes will be easier on her knees, as well as a new floor and air-conditioning and heating systems. It also means staff can schedule vacations without worrying about leaving the kitchen stretched for help.

Right now, however, Clemens has come downstairs to discuss with Edgar which cake they should cut from the rotation to make room for the Lemon Cloud. The Lemon Cloud and Strawberry Blossom cakes are both seasonal to spring and summer. Clemens thinks they should begin cutting the Chocolate Mousse immediately, but Edgar has already prepped the Mousse because he saw the case upstairs was empty. They agree after this round they'll switch to the Lemon Cloud. She then heads upstairs to discuss soda bread for St. Patrick's Day with Roman. "We only do it one day a year, but people come from all over asking for it." She also plans to leave a note for the counter staff, reminding them to tell customers they need to pick up all their special orders on Saturday instead of Sunday. The Brooklyn St. Patrick's

Day Parade is being held on Sunday in the park, and it will be a nightmare for anyone trying to get to Ladybird by car.

Every Tuesday, Edgar makes the chocolate pudding that fills the Brooklyn Blackout. He makes five buckets, which requires five hours at the stove. Bakers spend hours standing in their kitchens each day, often in warm temperatures and with few breaks. The Ladybird staff adapts to these conditions in different ways. Edgar, for instance, wears Crocs to stay comfortable while on his feet; Mary Louise attends physical therapy regularly.

Edgar reels off baking stats to me as he wipes down his workplace. The Brooklyn Blackout is always four layers, except for the four-inch cakes that have three. Cakes larger than ten inches require a rim of fudge icing between the layers. Square cakes cost more because they require more filling. They also take more work to frost. I don't quite understand why this is until he removes the first special Blackout order from the fridge and places it on a white ceramic revolving cake stand. He places an eight-inch round Blackout that he filled yesterday on top, spinning the stand slowly and adjusting the cake so that it's perfectly centered. He then scoops up fudge with the spatula, drops it on the center of the cake and begins to spin the cake, spreading the frosting outward as he goes. He takes more icing and holds it against the side of the cake as it spins, spreading a thick, even layer all the way down to the bottom. Eventually he turns the spatula so the serrated edge is against the icing, making thin, level ridges around the side and across the top. If this were a rectangular cake he'd obviously be unable to spin it, increasing the time and precision it would take to properly frost.

Before he began frosting, Edgar had sliced a thin layer off the top of the cake to make it completely flat. I assumed that the leftover would be tossed, but it turns out these discarded Blackout cake tops go into trays above the workstation to dry. Once dry, they'll be taken upstairs and ground into crumbs. There's nothing to indicate how long these thin, uneven slices have been out—no sort of timer or date attached to the tray—but Edgar can tell just by looking at them not just how long they've been sitting, but whether they're ready to be blended. He points to the top tray and shakes his head. "Too dry." If the crumbs are too dry, then the cake won't look fresh, he says. I tell him I can't see a difference between any of the trays. He assures me one is at the perfect level of dryness and the others are too moist. "Fifteen years working here, you can tell."

He goes upstairs to blend the chosen tray, and returns a few minutes later with a mountain of crumbs. He places the tray beside the Blackout that is still on the stand, and begins to slowly spin the stand as he scoops up enormous handfuls of crumbs and presses them onto the side of the cake until it is entirely covered. He then takes out the pastry tube of fudge icing and rims the cake with it. This cake is for a special order and needs extra decorating, so it goes back into the fridge until Pedro can get to it. Pedro does the special frosting every day except Friday, when Clemens takes over. This limited schedule is a nod to the physical toll baking can take on a body. After all these years of standing, Clemens's knees can no longer hold up to the hours required to decorate cakes, even though she is quick to emphasize she still loves that part of her job and relishes the times she gets to do it.

As Edgar opens the fridge door I once again get a whiff of the special smell the Blackouts give off, a mixture of cake, frosting, and—possibly—magic.

"That smells amazing," I say to Edgar.

"I don't smell a thing," says Edgar, matter of factly.

Edgar thinks if I worked here just one day I'd get tired of the Blackout. I'm fairly certain it would take more than a day, but I begin to get a better understanding of what he means when he immediately pulls out a tray of nearly a dozen Blackout cakes that haven't been filled yet and begins to line them up on his workstation; everywhere I look there are Blackouts. He methodically drops a scoop of pudding in the middle, spreading it and placing another layer of cake and pudding on top, and then again, and then again, until there are three more filled Blackouts. These go back into the fridge to set. They'll get frosted later. And then he does it again and again and again.

Every once in a while, Edgar stops to stretch. His neck bothers him from standing for hours at the same angle, as does his shoulder from holding the spatula day in and day out. I suggest he consider trying a yoga class; he smiles at me skeptically.

If BAKING IS A great math equation, then each cake is a construction project. For example, the ten-inch Brooklyn Blackouts need a ring of fudge icing around each layer. Without these rings, the weight of the top layers would become too heavy, collapse, and push the precious pudding out the sides of the cake. This is physics, basic weight distribution; the same rules determine the stable construction of buildings as well as cakes. This is also true for jelly-filled cakes, which also get a rim of buttercream on the outside; like peanut butter on a sandwich, the buttercream prevents the jelly from leaking.

Edgar now lays out four rows of four-inch Yellow cake layers, five to each row. Before he starts, he slices the top of some of the cakes. These cakes are all going in the display case and need to appear uniform in size. Of these twenty cakes, five will be filled with jelly, ten with pastry cream, and five with fudge.

"The fudge dries out the fastest," Edgar says, so he uses it up first.

Once he's ready to move on to the jelly-filled cakes, I open the timer on my phone and hit START. As the numbers start to roll by, I watch his hands move nearly as quickly. He creates a buttercream circle on the outside, adds a scoop of jam in the middle, and spreads it out before stacking it on the cake layer in line below it. He slides the spatula around the outside to ensure it's smooth. Done. Next. He repeats this process for each cake. It takes him only ninety seconds to do all of the five jelly-filled cakes. Once properly filled, all twenty cakes go back in the fridge to chill. Once they're chilled, the fudge-filled one will be frosted in fudge, and the jelly and pastry cream cakes will be frosted in buttercream.

Next up are the Yellow cakes he filled earlier this morning while I was upstairs. He sets a new bowl of buttercream under the mixer to soften so he can spread. Before frosting the cakes, he peels back the edge of the circular cardboard tray they sit on and writes the name of the filling inside each cake: jam, fudge, pastry. Each of these cakes are the same size and will be frosted in buttercream; there's no way for the staff behind the counter to know what's inside unless Edgar writes it down before he frosts.

The iPhone has now switched from the pregame to a comedy show in Spanish as Edgar places the first cake on the revolving stand. I start the timer on my phone again as he takes a scoop of the now soft buttercream and begins to spread it around the cake. Buttercream is trickier than fudge; it's more delicate and more difficult to make look polished. I watch as he spreads the white frosting around, scooping and swirling and spreading, not wasting even the tiniest smear until the entire six-inch cake is perfectly covered. I stop the clock.

"It took you a minute and fifteen seconds to frost that," I tell him.

"Really?" He raises his eyebrows and grins. "I think I'm good."

Roman comes downstairs to change back into his regular clothes. He'll head home now to be in bed by 7:00 p.m. so he can be up at 2:00 a.m. to make the trip back here. It's also time for me to leave. I take my apron off and toss it into the big basket Edgar points to. I ask him how much he has left to do. He walks me back to the fridge and opens the door. Again, that smell. The fridge is full of all the naked Blackouts that I saw earlier this morning.

"I have to frost all of these," says Edgar. I ask how many that is. He says there are seventy-two four-inch, sixty six-inch, and eighteen eight-inch cakes, all waiting for the touch of his spatula to make them complete.

"Wow," I say.

He shrugs with a grin. "Every week is the same."

THE APPRENTICE ROUTE EDGAR took through baking is still one followed today by those who opt out of attending professional schools like the CIA or San Francisco Baking Institute, or find themselves somewhat accidentally in the baking world.

As mentioned, Clemens is a graduate of CIA and sees its benefits. "It was very useful. I learned all aspects of cooking, not just baking. Also just being in so many commercial kitchens and being around other people with different backgrounds; it gave me a confidence." Even so, she thinks that with the present-day realities of tuition—which have increased exponentially since her time there—the apprenticeship model makes a great deal of sense.

"Nowadays I think people really need to think hard about what they want, because I've known people that have gone to CIA since I got out, and it's like the ratio of people getting back what they put in. You need to have some expertise, but if you're locked into a really great apprenticeship, you might be better off with that. But you've got to get a really great apprenticeship."

This was exactly what Hannah Martin fell into when they (Martin prefers the gender pronouns *they* and *them*) started out working behind the counter at Jesse and Kit's Sea Wolf bakery in Seattle. In fact, it was partly the idea of a repetitive physical routine that drew Martin from the front of house to the back.

At twenty-two years old, Martin was working as an assistant at a law firm while finishing their undergraduate degree in English. Initially hopeful that the job would provide enough free time to pursue their writing, they soon found themselves bored and miserable, filing papers, making copies, endlessly calling insurance companies. Says Martin, "It was a lot of stapling. I got really good at removing staples." As they began their job search, they recalled how much they'd enjoyed the one-on-one contact with people they'd experienced in a past job as a wedding photographer and, hoping to replicate that feeling, took a position working the counter at Sea Wolf temporarily until they found something else that aligned more closely with their goals.

The bakery had only just opened and was still in the process of finding its footing. From their vantage, they had a catbird seat to everything the bakers in the back were doing. Sea Wolf has an open setup, so even the customers have a full view of everything the bakers do in the kitchen. Over the course of their first year, Martin was able to see what a day for a baker actually looked like, the constraints they were working with, and the rhythm of the kitchen, and became increasingly enamored with what the bakers were doing. One of the advantages of working in a business that is just beginning to grow is that it can be very all-hands-on-deck. As Sea Wolf became busier and moved into a seven-day schedule, Martin frequently found themself being asked to pick up some back-of-house tasks, like pulling bread from the oven or assisting in shaping a loaf; they were fascinated by the entire process. They mentioned their interest to Kit and Jesse, and the next time a position opened in the back the brothers moved them right in.

"I was very clear I had no prior experience," says Martin. This sort of from-the-bottom-up, on-the-ground training—the kind that dates back to the beginning of baking—is one still available to bakers who opt not to go to the cooking-school route. And can have the advantage of dropping would-be bakers into the deep end of responsibilities very quickly.

"I didn't know anything about sourdough, for instance," says Martin, "but Kit and Jesse were very adamant that it was something you could learn and be trained up into it." Or, catapulted into. In very short order Martin found themself in the role of the mixer, which required them to do all the doughs for an entire day's bake, as well as the day's shaping. At many bakeries this would be considered a senior role, a revered position, since the quality and shape of the dough is what determines the entire baking process.

"It was very intimidating," recalls Martin. "I didn't know what dough was supposed to look like. Is it too tough, did I

Kneading dough

mix it a minute too long, is it going to be too loose, should I add another fold?"

At the same time, they found the immense challenges exhilarating. "You're constantly asking questions, talking to the bakers." Here, too, the repetition that Edgar reflected on as challenging in the long-term—the doing of the same thing day in and day out—paid off for Martin in a steep learning curve. They quickly learned how to touch the dough and know if it was ready, to hold it up to the light and see if it hung down in a proper "window." There is a language and lexicon that comes with baking, and the more they got their hands on the dough the more they were able to employ it. "It's exciting to know enough about a trade that you're aware of your own inadequacies." Experiments were also welcome at Sea Wolf; sometimes Martin would come in and find dough simply marked KIT and knew there would be "something interesting happening later."

Kit and Jesse's habit of printing out and posting an article or essay or various scientific information about bread, following it up the next day with another three-page article tacked to the whiteboard explaining it, also sped up their education. By the time they were fully trained a few months later, Martin was working four days a week, either shape shifts or bake shifts from 5:00 a.m. to 3:00 p.m., or the pastry shift from 4:00 a.m. to 2:00 p.m. By this point, the physical toll baking exacts on the body had ceased to be the surprise it had been in the beginning.

"It was actually remarkable to see my body transform over the course of not really intending it to," says Martin. "The first month that I worked the back of house, I was constantly exhausted. But it became a really gratifying process, especially when I worked the mix station, just because you get to be really intimate with the dough, and you get to be really intimate with the process. You come in very early, and you start the day by moving around fifty-pound flour bags, or getting all of your bins ready, or you're constantly folding the dough and lifting it, and it was sometimes in the middle of the summer when it's ninety degrees in the bakery, and you look at the clock and you're like, 'Oh, it's not even six a.m., and I'm already sweating.' But it was really gratifying."

The most gratifying part, Martin says, was the thrill of inserting themself into a profession that has existed largely unchanged for hundreds and hundreds of years. "I'm making my way into this grand lineage, this process, and I have just a tiny, tiny bit of knowledge, enough to know that there's so much that I need to understand."

8

THE FUTURE OF BAKING

Baking is everywhere these days. Even if you're not a baker or have even minimal interest in it, it's likely you'll come across something baking related on a fairly regular basis. The emergence of baking as a cultural force, some might even argue obsession, is tied to a number of things. First perhaps is that it's satisfying, and not just to consume.

Sometime in late 2018, as I was scrambling to finish writing a book that refused to be finished, I turned to Netflix in search of some programming. I did not want a series that would suck me in and refuse to let me go. I wanted something pleasant, but that was also resistant to bingeing. In the past, *Friends* had provided this refuge, but I wanted even *less* narrative. Something like a nature documentary, maybe about plants. I don't recall what search terms I entered, but one of the top results was *The Great British Bake*

Off (*GBBO*), retitled *The Great British Baking Show* stateside. It seemed innocent enough.

I had heard mention of *GBBO* in passing over the years, scrolled by comments about it in my Twitter feed, and knew people were enjoying it, beyond that it belonged to a segment of entertainment I'd never bothered with, in fact avoided might be more accurate: I'd never seen a cooking show, or even a reality TV show for that matter. Moreover, the *GBBO* thumbnail on my screen contained a certain absurdity to it—four people, none under forty, holding up a cake. One looked like she might be impersonating Queen Elizabeth II, one looked like an aging British rock star from the late seventies. One looked like she might have just been gardening. And one looked like George Clooney with white hair and a beard. It was very, very British. Beyond that, how interesting could baking be?

Famous last words, as they say.

I started at the end, simply because that's what started playing first, and worked my way backward. Before the end of the week I had binged three seasons of the show, living and dying along with Kim-Joy when her decorations didn't work out. Holding my breath with Rahul when his chocolate castle didn't melt and clapping my hands with surprised joy after steely blue-eyed judge Paul Hollywood (aka white-haired George Clooney) thrust out his hand to Manon for a coveted shake. Was there anything quite so cruel as Prue (the Queen's look-alike) tasting the *slimmest* slice of cake and quietly saying, "I'm disappointed. I can hardly taste the gin," or Ruby pulling open the drawer to discover the bread hadn't proved enough. THE BREAD HAD NOT PROVED ENOUGH. I wasn't exactly sure how one was supposed to gauge a properly proved bread, but by the time I'd reached the tenth episode I knew its failure to do so was nothing short of Shakespearean.

Apart from being amazed that baking could be so *dramatic*, there was something extremely assuring, almost nourishing, about watching people compete to accomplish a feat that was dictated by such a specific set of rules.

The first thing anyone will tell you about baking is that it's incredibly precise, mathematical. Baking requires precision. There aren't many rule breakers in baking, few, if any risk-takers. Baking requires an attention to detail and a respect for the laws of science. How moist is the air? How will that affect the dough? Is the cake rising? There are no fixing things if the cake doesn't rise. No amount of adventurous flavoring makes a flat cake taste better; there is no option for wild experimentation with olive oil and rough handfuls of chopped garlic. But this also means that baking is open to anyone who can follow a recipe. If cooking is an adventure, baking is a highly coordinated military operation; you can march along just fine, but step out of line and you're done for.

These are, to put it mildly, chaotic times that we live in. The world can seem wildly out of our control and relentlessly intruding into our lives. There is something deeply comforting about the idea of knowing, *knowing*, that 3 cups all-purpose or bread flour (more for dusting), ¼ teaspoon instant yeast, 1¼ teaspoons salt plus some cornmeal for coating a towel (*not* terry cloth) will, if you follow the instructions, result in Jim Lahey's famous no-knead bread.

Bea Arthur, a New York City–based therapist, says this return to baking, particularly in the encroaching digital era, makes complete sense and aligns with what she and other therapists are seeing in their practice. "We have a really high consumer culture now," says Arthur. She says that high "consumption, especially with constant content, and reading and receiving" is then paired with our natural passive state. The extra complication, she says, is that this passive state conflicts with our psyche "because a lot of what we see on the internet makes us angry. We're in a passive state, but we're activating anger, which is not the best place to be. You're not doing anything with that energy."

Activities like baking allow us to focus. While baking, we're able to drown out that constant content and pay attention to the task at hand. Baking also "activates our creativity," says Arthur. "The opposite of consumption is creating. Making something with your hands, seeing it through. You're just focused on the directions, and then you have a really nice treat. [Creation] really activates all of your reward systems. It activates all of your basic needs that sitting around on your phone and consuming just don't."

For millennials, an endlessly discussed generation largely raised on the internet, who are getting married later, working longer hours, and living with less financial security than their parents, these are no small things. *The Atlantic* published a piece in 2018 noting that millennials' lack of cooking skills has been well documented but what gets lost in that well-trod fact is that lack of meals around the table also means lack of community. *Real* community, the kind that gathers to break bread together.

"I call myself the cake historian," says Jessica Reed, "but baking has changed so much over the past few years that I've broadened my studies to include the mental health–

identity aspects of exploring baked goods." Baking, she notes, can center you, but it is also tangible evidence of not being centered. "I recently myself have had one of the worst cake sales in my life because I was trying to do too many things at once and I was distracted. To really do it effectively you have to pay attention so that gets you into that meditative state which calms you down and then you actually, you get the pride of producing something. You've made something and it's something that is purely meant to provide happiness."

Reed also thinks some of this desire for simplicity is what drives both the *Great British Bake Off*'s appeal and our desire to replicate it. "For years and years and years the TV shows were having you create a cake that doesn't look like a cake. People were making cakes that look like the Empire State Building or look like a dog or whatever, and now I think there's been—and *The Great British Baking Show* is an excellent example, but even before that—a return to a more humble baking. More what-your-grandmother-would-bake kind of baking, which I think is more accessible for people."

But for those who shy away from baking or running a bakery as a full-time profession, there are other avenues into similar careers, some of which offer an alternative to the physical toll full-time baking can take on the body.

Luisa Weiss, who pens *The Wednesday Chef* blog and wrote the memoir, *My Berlin Kitchen*, briefly considered becoming a baker. She spent one Saturday in the kitchen at Amy's Bread, a New York City institution, before realizing the work was so hard and relentless it was the equivalent of "laying bricks."

Instead, Weiss, who now lives in Berlin with her husband and two children, eventually satisfied her baking urges by writing *Classic German Baking*. Published in 2016, it required its own sort of endurance, far less than running a bakery. Getting the recipes polished for publication entailed baking pastries over and over again until they were perfected. Entries "were tested upward of ten times," with the average being six. Considering there are more than a hundred recipes in her cookbook, the research and development process was intense and time-consuming. "We would make a cake and then I'd cut a sliver of cake and then cut it in half. At a certain point, you only need a bite or two to figure out whether it's okay."

The repetition was offset by what Weiss describes as a larger purpose with the book. "I wasn't just trying to come up [with ideas], you know. None of these recipes were mine. I was getting them from places. My goal with the book was to deliver this slice of an aspect of German culture to the American market. I felt like that was the bigger engine driving me forward." But, she wonders, how do bakeries come up with new ideas? How do they contribute to their communities while staying relevant and profitable? How do they do it?

How THEY DO IT and why they do it are questions a new generation of bakers seems to be asking itself more frequently. Perhaps it's not surprising that the onset of social media has created an entirely new sort of baker. Let's call them the performing bakers. Or what Reed terms "lifestyle bakers."

One need only to glance at the cake hashtag on Instagram or Pinterest to behold the performing baker. These are not people who are making vast amounts of product to sell. They're not concerned with profit margins and leftover goods. Nor are they necessarily worried about taste. These bakers are concerned solely with the appearance of their baked creations. Which makes these cakes, cupcakes, pies, and tarts distant relatives of the confections that in centuries past graced the tables of kings and queens, which were made to last for weeks and never be consumed. Additionally, these bakers are often making one flawless, extravagant, gorgeous cake in order to post one perfect picture, which can garner thousands of likes and possible sponsorships for the baker. There's a similar industry on YouTube, where you can find hundreds of instructional cake-decorating videos.

The social media craze is an offshoot of what began as the cooking-show craze dating back to Julia Child's first appearance on the screen. Shows like *Cake Boss* and *Ace of Cakes* heralded the rise of baked goods during the general rise of televised, competitive food culture. The types of extravagant baking that began on these shows a decade ago have since migrated to the social media masses. Food as theatrical performance. Unicorn cupcakes, cakes made to look like Disney characters, pies with Beyoncé's face baked into them. Cakes adorned with feminist creeds and others adorned with Drake's lyrics—the list is somewhat endless. As are the occasions. It's also, Reed notes, a kind of baking that "fuels dreams" instead of people.

"You're not baking for your kid's birthday or for your

church bake sale. You're not baking to have a bakery. You're baking to fuel the daydreams of people." Reed notes that her gateway drug, as it were, into cakes was simply the pictures of cakes. "I had a blog twelve years ago called *Pictures of Cakes* that was just for me. I was so miserable at work, and I wanted a place full of pictures of cakes because that made me feel happy."

She thinks it's much the same impulse that drives the baking phenomenon on social media. "There's just something nice and cozy and pleasing about seeing a well-styled cake. I think most people attribute cakes with happiness and with celebration and with warmth and love." In the past, this sort of editorial would have been largely confined to the glossy pages of a magazine. These days, the social media world—and all the highly stylized photos fit to filter—is open to anyone who understands how to capitalize on it.

"It's a huge change," says Reed. "There are bakers who work through blogs and Instagram alone, and are making a fortune. And they're just home bakers. They are baking this right in their kitchen, they are photographing them beautifully, and they're not making necessarily anything all that different than what other people are making. And social media is fueling the commerce. Social media is driving not only the accessibility of these things to a wider range of people but it's also powering an economy in a way."

Elisa Strauss, a cake designer who runs a company called Confetti Cakes and now teaches classes and consults on cakes, started out designing cakes for corporations that cost upward of ten thousand dollars. What does such an expensive cake look like, you might ask?

"We did a Victorian house. We matched the paint chips from the house to the cake, and they had hydrangeas out front. We did a Lego Batman thing for Warner Brothers. I did something for MoMA, a Claes Oldenburg replica. I was replicating things." She hit the big time when one of her cakes was featured on *Sex and the City* as Charlotte and Harry's wedding cake. But even then, it was a struggle, and she knew she needed to adapt her business model.

"I saw the writing on the wall very early. You just can't have a life and also run a cake business. All of my friends who are still cake designers, they either started it much later, like after they had children, or they're men and women that have just dedicated their life to the kitchen instead of a family. There was no way for me to have a balanced life. I work 24/7. So I started teaching and, to the same point as social media, it was like, 'Oh wait, I actually know what my schedule is, and I can charge just as much.' It was like a better business model."

Strauss understands the appeal of the social media baker from that standpoint. The bigger the audience, the more sponsorship you get. In the twenty-first century, it's possible to be a baker while baking things that no one will actually purchase. "Every day, *every day* I get emails from people," says Strauss. "I'm not even that successful. I have fifty thousand followers on YouTube. I haven't posted a tutorial in over a year. People who are doing tutorials every week—if not three times a week—are getting the same emails from products that will pay you for Instagram. One post, one story, one blog post, or whatever. I get those all the time. So for someone starting their business, if they get into a pattern of that, then that can be their whole business. They don't need the bakery. They don't need to deal with employees, they don't need to deal with worker's comp and insurance."

BACK AT LADYBIRD, HOWEVER, Clemens has little interest in social media or baking books or "influencers" as far as they go. It's enough to know the cakes go out and are enjoyed and the customers return. The physical toll of baking, however, is something Clemens thinks about a lot and believes every baker should take into serious consideration. Her lease on the space Ladybird occupies is up for renewal this summer, and she's been giving serious consideration to letting the business go. She's careful to do her physical therapy and has started going to Pilates, but has to limit her time in the kitchen to no more than five hours one or two times a week. Still, would she be able to keep this up? That was her overriding concern at the end of a quarter century in the business.

In the end, she decided to stay put. Instead, she shuffled the kitchen around so that Gregario, the dishwasher, would move into a baking role, allowing Roman and Edgar to take on more of the decorating and keep her time on her feet to an absolute minimum.

"Now we just need to find a dishwasher," she says with a sigh. "Which is not easy!"

"The truth is, I just love it," Clemens says. "I always tell everybody who works for me, everybody who thinks they want to be a baker: You have to bake all day and be on your feet and go home and still want to bake something at home. You're always seeking out that thing that's going to be new or different or right for the occasion. That's also the thing, what's right for the thing. So, you just have to just love it. You're never going to get rich. You're not going to get famous."

Nicole Cramer concurs. "You open a bakery for the love of baking and sharing," she says, emailing after spending twenty hours a day for three straight days of Passover and Easter holiday madness on her feet. "Not for the love of fame or money."

"We're here at three in the morning," says Clemens. "We're here on holidays. We're here not spending it with our family on a holiday, and we're exhausted with our families on the holiday, so everybody else can celebrate their holiday. You have to love it."

APPENDIX

Deciding to become a baker, or even simply exploring a curiosity in the profession, is made both easier and more challenging by the fact that a formal education or degree is not required. Easier because if tuition is out of your reach it is very possible, as a number of people featured in this book have done, to find a position in a bakery and work (the old-school term for it is apprentice) your way up the ladder, gaining experience in various areas while being paid to do so.

Should a formal education appeal, however, perhaps because there are no viable bakeries or positions accessible to you, or even because you prefer the structure, instruction, or connections a school might offer, there are numerous programs around the country dedicated to instructing students in the culinary arts (examples noted in this book include the Culinary Institute of America, the Institute of Culinary Education, and the International Culinary Center). Even with the downsizing of culinary programs around the country, a quick Google search will reveal hundreds of classes and courses being offered in a variety of topics and skill sets at colleges near you.

For those who are interested in pursuing baking outside a professional setting there's no shortage of baking books out there. The following books come recommended by some of the people profiled in this book, as well as titles that were mentioned repeatedly over the course of researching and writing. They provide a variety of perspectives on and guides to baking, including recipes, history, and science.

- *The Cake Bible* (New York: HarperCollins, 1988), *The Bread Bible* (New York: W. W. Norton, 2003), and *The Baking Bible* (New York: Houghton Mifflin Harcourt, 2014), by Rose Levy Baranbaum

   Considered classics in the baking world (*The Cake Bible* is in its fifty-fourth printing), these award-winning *Bibles* provide recipes and lessons on the chemistry of baking, and explain the importance of various techniques.

- *On Food and Cooking: The Science and Lore of the Kitchen* (New York: Scribner, revised edition 2004) by Harold McGee

  Considered the modern bible of baking, this nearly nine-hundred-page book is a combination of recipes, historical anecdotes, diagrams, explainers, and science.

- *Bread: A Baker's Book of Techniques and Recipes* (Hoboken: John Wiley & Sons, second edition 2013) by Jeffery Hamelman

  Geared toward professionals and amateurs alike, Hamelman provides recipes for a wide array of breads, providing formulas, science, and stories.

- *The Baker's Appendix: The Essential Kitchen Companion, with Deliciously Dependable, Infinitely Adaptable Recipes* (New York: Clarkson Potter, 2017) by Jessica Reed

  An exhaustive reference guide, which includes metric conversion and extensive ingredient variations.

- *Ratio: The Simple Codes Behind the Craft of Everyday Cooking* (New York: Scribner, 2009) by Michael Ruhlman

  This book takes baking as math to its most extreme conclusion. Ruhlman breaks recipes down into ratios, and uses them as the launching point to explore substitutions and variations.

- *Classic German Baking: The Very Best Recipes for Traditional Favorites, from Pfeffernüsse to Streuselkuchen* (New York: Ten Speed Press, 2016) by Luisa Weiss

  Weiss collects traditional German baking recipes, many of which have been passed along through generations, tested and geared toward an American audience.

- *My Life in France* (New York: Knopf, 2006) by Julia Child with Alex Prud'homme

  Child's classic and delightful memoir of her life in France after the war and how she came to cooking.

ABOUT THE AUTHOR

Glynnis MacNicol is a writer and cofounder of TheLi.st. MacNicol is the author of the memoir *No One Tells You This* and cowrote *Hello Flo: The Guide, Period* with HelloFlo founder Naama Bloom. Her work has appeared in print and online for publications including Elle.com (where she was a contributing writer), *The New York Times*, *The Guardian*, *Forbes*, *The Cut*, *New York Daily News*, *W*, *Town & Country*, and *The Daily Beast*. "From the Ground Up," her five-part series on the Brownsville neighborhood in Brooklyn, won a 2015 Contently Award. She lives in New York City.